63 Days and a Wake-Up

63 Days and a Wake-Up

Your Survival Guide to United States Army Basic Combat Training

Don Herbert

iUniverse, Inc.
New York Lincoln Shanghai

63 Days and a Wake-Up
Your Survival Guide to United States Army Basic Combat Training

iUniverse books may be ordered through booksellers or by contacting:

iUniverse
2021 Pine Lake Road, Suite 100
Lincoln, NE 68512
www.iuniverse.com
1-800-Authors (1-800-288-4677)

Because of the dynamic nature of the Internet, any Web addresses or links contained in this book may have changed since publication and may no longer be valid.

The views expressed in this work are solely those of the author and do not necessarily reflect the views of the publisher, and the publisher hereby disclaims any responsibility for them.

Cover Photo Credits

Front cover photograph: Staff Sergeant Clayton Bowen, a Drill Sergeant with the 193rd Infantry Brigade, 1st Battalion, 13th Infantry Regiment, Bravo Company, Fort Jackson, South Carolina, provides outstanding instruction to his soldiers in the operation of the M249 Squad Automatic Weapon (SAW). Photograph and graphics by the author.

Back cover photographs: Drill Sergeant Bowen demonstrates the use of the AT-4 anti-tank weapon. Private Bobby Hill, assigned to the 193rd Infantry Brigade, 1st Battalion, 34th Infantry Regiment, Alpha Company, Fort Jackson, South Carolina, negotiates the Individual Movement and Technique (IMT) range. Private Hill also earned two honors for his Company as the Soldier Leader of the Cycle and High EOC-APFT. Photographs by Dan Powers. Graphics by the author.

ISBN: 978-0-595-42511-2

Printed in the United States of America

The writing of this book would not have been possible if it weren't for those before me who fought and died for my right to do so. It's tragic how the right to free speech is often used to denigrate those who defend that right, when it should be used to honor those who provide such a privilege.

And that's what this book is all about: helping those who are willing to defend, at all costs our families, our liberty, and our way of life. Freedom, while defined in the Constitution, is not a right, nor guaranteed and must be defended in battle. And that, whether we like it or not, spells duty.

Serving my country has always been one of my passions. It is truly a privilege and an honor to serve beside one of the bravest, most selfless generations in American history. I have always held those who pioneered my freedom in reverence.
My heroes now include those who provide it to others.

So here's to the men and women of the United States, past, present, and future, who've heard the call, risen to the challenge, met their destinies, and earned the distinction that few ever will:

American Soldier.
★ ★ ★ ★ ★ ★ ★ ★

Contents

Acknowledgments

I've come to realize that the writing of a book is not possible without the help of others, some of whom had paid, professional responsibilities to assist and others who owed me nothing and could have refused my requests, but didn't. Although I bear sole responsibility for the content of this book, I would be remiss if I were to accept all of the praise for the work myself. I believe in giving credit where credit is due. I would like to thank the following people for helping to make this book possible:

God, for everything. My wife, Alissa, for the brilliant decision to marry me. I don't know what she was thinking, but it's too late now! I'm nothing without her. My children, Chris, Hannah, and Olivia, for their constant reminders of what really matters. My father and mother, Don and Christine, and the rest of the Herbert clan, for their love and continued support, for which I am so fortunate. I hope I always make you proud. My father-in-law and mother-in-law, Ron and Judy Ward, for raising such a fine daughter and for accepting me into their family. Dan Powers, CEMF, Devil Dog, and all-around good guy, for being one of the few people I can always count on. The world needs more good men like you. Ms. Aileen Ciesla, for agreeing on such short notice to be photographed for the fitness section. Lieutenant Colonel Kevin Cooney, Captain Neysa Burkes, Command Sergeant Major Marion Mike, First Sergeant Joseph Dilks, Drill Sergeants Blue, Bowen, Case, Cooke, Deberry, Johnson, Lytle, Osorio, Rivers, Taylor, and Wilburn, 193rd Infantry Brigade, 1st Battalion, 13th Infantry Regiment, Bravo Company, Fort Jackson, South Carolina, for their hard work and dedication during BCT and for their hospitality during my media visit while writing this book. I was lucky to have been one of their soldiers-in-training, and I am humbled to wear the same uniform. They are what makes America great. Captain Patrick LaChance and First Lieutenant Christopher Myer, 193rd Infantry Brigade, 1st Battalion, 34th Infantry Regiment, Alpha Company, Fort Jackson, South Carolina, for allowing us to take pictures of their soldiers-in-training on the IMT course. We're lucky to have such fine men leading troops. Ms. Julia Simpkins, Mr. James Hinnant, and Lieutenant Colonel Jeff Buczkowski, U.S. Army Public Affairs, for allowing me photographic access to soldiers-in-training at Fort Jackson, South Carolina. First Sergeant David Bobenmoyer and the cadre of Bravo Company, Recruit Sustainment

Battalion, Camp Grayling, Michigan, for their hard work and dedication in preparing soldiers for success at BCT and AIT and for living the example of how NCO's should mentor their soldiers. Chief Steve Ronk and the men and women of Independence Fire Department, Clarkston, Michigan, for their support in my quest to become an American soldier. I am blessed to be part of such a great organization and to be surrounded by fine people. Staff Sergeant Adam Buttel, U.S. Army Recruiter, for being crazy enough to allow the Army to enlist me. He'll live to regret it one day. The Staff at iUniverse Publishing, Lincoln, Nebraska, for answering my incessant and inane questions and for their professionalism in making my first publishing experience a pleasant one.

Answering the Call

It's been a long time since my first experience with military preparatory training at Fort Jackson, South Carolina: June of 1956 to be exact. In my fifty years of service, irrespective of capacitance, I have had the wonderful experience of working with Basic Combat Training graduates either in active Army service, with the National Guard, or the Tennessee State Guard. These are indeed the finest men and women America has to offer.

The emotional awakening to service, duty, and patriotism of America's soldiers begins at different times and in different forms for prospective soldiers. Some gather it externally from friends and family members who have served. Others gain it through an internal mechanism which recognizes that we owe the debt of duty for the sacrifices of the men and women that secured our freedom.

63 Days and a Wake-Up will provide you with the essential basic knowledge that, in most cases, you didn't even realize you needed. As I read the book I realized that although times may have changed since my initial entry training, nothing has really changed in the required skills and motivation, both learned and developed, to complete basic military training. The work contained in the following pages is timeless. Specialist Herbert has provided many outstanding bits of advice gained from recent experience that will make your training experience worthwhile and facilitate a better use of the training time available. I also suggest parents or significant others of the prospective soldier read this primer as well.

As a new soldier-in-training, the first best thing to arm yourself with is knowledge. Those of us who have already experienced the training realize the value of an old Army axiom known as the "Five P's": Prior Planning Prevents Poor Performance! Complete this book and then complete BCT, and you will know and understand fully that old axiom.

Major General (TN) William E. "Whit" Whitworth, Sr. 20 August 2007

General Whitworth is a highly decorated multi-era Army veteran. His service started with his enlistment in the United States Army in 1956. His professional military education includes the Air Force Command and Staff College, The Armor Officer

Advanced Course, The Infantry Officer Candidate School (OCS), the Armor Advanced Non-Commissioned Officer Academy and both fixed and rotary wing flight training. General Whitworth's first assignment was with the 11th Air Assault Division during the testing of air/land warfare concepts and armed helicopters. He served two tours in Vietnam, serving with the 101st Airborne Division, and numerous other aviation units. He specialized in Attack Helicopter warfare and commanded the army's first Attack Helicopter unit. He has additionally worked many military cartographic and mapping issues during a tour with the Defense Mapping Agency. He retired from the active Regular Army as a Lieutenant Colonel in October 1988. Since that time, he has served either with the Army National Guard, or the Tennessee State Guard. General Whitworth is married to the former Sandra Cook of Jackson, Georgia and they live in Jefferson City, Tennessee. General Whitworth is an employee of the State of Tennessee as a Program Coordinator with the Program Review Unit, Office of the Inspector General, Department of Human Services.

Caveat

This book was written by the author as an independent endeavor. Though reviews have been written by current and retired Army soldiers, and while some of you had your Recruiters recommend this book to you, that should not be construed as a formal endorsement by the United States Army.

In the name of security for our armed forces personnel, specific training methods, places, schedules, and equipment will go without mention. The bad guys can get their information from somewhere else.

Before beginning any exercise program, you should consult your doctor and obtain his or her approval or receive approval from the physician during the medical evaluation (physical) at MEPS.

All pictures, graphics, and tables appearing herein are the sole property of the author unless otherwise notated. Pictures of soldiers-in-training were taken with permission and under the escort and supervision of the Army Public Affairs Office at Fort Jackson, South Carolina.

Current preparatory training programs, requirements, incentives, and other benefits mentioned in this book may change without notice. A Recruiter will have an updated list of what the Army has to offer.

Updates, corrections, and retractions will be posted on my Web site, www.63daysandawakeup.com.

Unless specified otherwise, no part of this book shall be reproduced without the express, written consent of the author. For requests, questions, and concerns or to report an error in content, please email don@63daysandawakeup.com.

No soldiers were harmed in the making of this book. However, a few Marines were severely teased ... from a comfortable distance.

Introduction

What It's All About

63 Days and a Wake-Up is a survival guide—a primer—designed to:

- ⊕ answer the most frequently asked questions about BCT;
- ⊕ take you inside the world of the Army, explaining the civilian-to-soldier transformation process, starting with recruitment and ending with your graduation from BCT;
- ⊕ provide sound advice for both male and female soldiers through real-time experiences, helping you avoid common pitfalls that can affect your training performance;
- ⊕ offer insider information on what makes your Drill Sergeants tick and, more importantly, what you can do to avoid setting them off;
- ⊕ help you identify weaknesses—physical, mental, administrative, and financial—and provide solutions, so you can turn them into strengths before heading down-range for training;
- ⊕ illustrate and explain the components of the Army Physical Fitness Test and teach you proper exercise form, so you can obtain your best possible score in each APFT event;
- ⊕ provide an illustrated basic physical fitness guide and training program, helping you get into "Army shape" prior to shipping to BCT.

Why It Was Written

The main inspiration for this book is you: the soon-to-be American soldier, guardian of freedom and exporter of liberty. I have personally witnessed many soldiers suffer unnecessarily through BCT because they were mentally and physically unprepared for the rigors of training. Many of them were also administratively incorrect, meaning that their paperwork was wrong. Those soldiers served as the inspiration for this book.

As of the writing of this book, United States Army Basic Combat Training (excluding the week at Reception Battalion) is nine weeks—*sixty-three days*—long. Nine weeks may seem like a long time, especially when viewed through the prism of your first week at BCT. But it will go by quickly, sometimes faster than you can keep up, if you're not prepared before you arrive.

What you'll find on the following pages is a survival guide, not step-by-step instructions. The citizen-to-soldier transformation will be one of the most challenging and difficult experiences of your life, but it will also be one of the most rewarding. The better-prepared you are for the change, the more you'll get out of BCT.

While the main focus of the book is on BCT itself, I would be remiss if I ignored the more personal aspects (finances, mental and physical preparation, etc.) that will have the greatest impact on your success and enjoyment of BCT. You'll have enough to bother about and keep up with during Basic without any unnecessary personal worries. This book will help you identify strengths, eliminate weaknesses, and solve potential problems prior to shipping to BCT.

I'm also not going to tell you every secret of Army BCT, because that would spoil all the fun! Some things just need to be experienced, and maintaining the element of surprise will keep you on your toes. Besides, there's no way to describe some of the madness of BCT, but it's safe to say that it's all good, some of it is fun, and it's all done for a reason.

Written in Real-Time

It is also important for you to know that the majority of this book was written while I was going through BCT in the summer of 2006. The project started out harmlessly enough as a small journal: a few random jottings that sprang to mind as I observed the new soldiers processing through Reception Battalion. At first, the problems they were experiencing seemed superficial but noteworthy enough to write a line or two about. I figured it would be good stuff to bring back to my Recruiter as a way of helping new recruits avoid such issues as they prepared to ship out to training.

But as training intensified, so did my note-taking, as there were plenty of soldiers who were obviously in over their heads, not because they were incapable, but because they clearly had no idea what they had gotten themselves into and it was too late to do anything about it. They all got through it but it wasn't pretty. Needless to say they gave me some great writing material. As I witnessed or experienced something, or after conversations with fellow soldiers-in-training (SIT), I made notes, and later (usually after lights-out), I would transcribe them onto a binder of paper. Unintentional as it was, my journal of advice quickly turned into a problem-solving instruction manual. And here we are today.

Where the Rubber Meets the Road

There is no logical way to write a book that includes the idiosyncrasies each training site holds for its soldiers-in-training. For instance, did you know that your main transport mode at Fort Jackson is a Blue Bird bus, but at Fort Benning, it's a cattle car? While this makes for great trivia, it's not the kind of information that's going to help you prepare for your training cycle, which is what this book is all about.

Having taken that into account, my advice on the following pages is specific to the essentials and easily applicable to whenever and wherever you serve your time in BCT. That's why this book and the information provided will prove itself as an indispensable resource to not only survive, but to excel in Army BCT.

The More Things Change, the More they Stay the Same

During the process of writing this book, I interviewed all the soldiers I could about their BCT experiences from World War II to the present. While warfare methodologies have most certainly changed due to technology, the training philosophy of basic soldiering from generation to generation has held remarkably steady. Many WWII, Korea, Vietnam, and Desert Storm veterans can still relate to many of the soldiering practices alive today in BCT. I've even had a WWII Paratrooper tell me, after his recent visit to Fort Benning, that the current airborne training program was harder than when he went through it.

There may be a social generational gap, but it narrows when the talk turns to soldiering, and that's a good thing. Maintaining the tradition of grit among American soldiers is crucial to continued respect and admiration for what each generation of soldier has sacrificed for their fellow man.

My Writing Style

No matter how interested I am in a particular subject, nothing turns me away from a book like an author who prattles on unnecessarily for several hundred pages. It remains a mystery to me why anyone would pen a book that by its very length defends itself against the risk of being read.

You won't find that here. If you're like me, you've got better things to do with your time and money than spend it on a three-hundred-page book that contains forty pages of substance. I believe in brevity, and I've made a concerted effort to make the following an easy read while keeping it substantive, without a lot of nattering. I promise it will be worth your time and money.

Not for Sale

This book exists for one primary reason: to offer honest insight based on my experiences and those of other soldiers, providing you with an unbiased, objective view of BCT. In short, I'm not going to try to "sell" the Army to you (that's your Recruiter's job). If you like what you read and it makes you more interested in joining, then fine. If you do not like what you read and it makes you less interested in joining, that's fine too. Regardless of what anyone tells you, and no matter how hard they try to convince you one way or the other, the decision to join must be yours alone. I'm just here to help you make an informed choice.

Mars and Venus

Some of you will attend training at an all-male BCT, like Fort Benning, while many of you will attend co-ed BCT. Unless otherwise notated, I make no distinction in my advice based on the gender of the soldier, because there is no difference in the training you'll receive or the tasks you'll be required to perform.

The Basics, Before Basic

Preparing Recruits for their initial training is not something that's new to me. As an instructor for the Fire Academy, I made it part of my job description to ensure that new students were prepared before they arrived for the start of the program. I developed a scaled-down version of a book like this for them to read before reporting to the five-week Academy.

This also meant meeting with them on a weekly basis to reinforce the fundamentals that they had read in the book and review the basics of the program, such as common terminology and definitions, the components of their protective equipment, familiarization with the tools of the trade, etc. Students who attended this preparatory training always had an easier time during the Academy than those who didn't and almost always scored better on their exams.

While I can provide the information, I obviously cannot physically meet with each of you to reaffirm and explain all the things I'm going to tell you. However, the Army offers formalized preparatory programs, and in the chapter "Go or Know-Go," I'll talk about the benefits of attending this type of preparatory training offered by your Recruiter before reporting to BCT. If you combine the knowledge you'll get from this book with your attendance at one of these preparatory programs, you'll report to BCT with a greater awareness and confidence, prepared for success.

Make the Investment, Reap the Benefits

Army BCT requires you to invest yourself: all of you, mind, body, and spirit. And like any investment; the greater the sacrifice, the bigger the return. BCT is treated by many as a stepping stone to their military careers, but it should be treated like a building block. After all, it's called *Basic*

Combat Training for a reason; your successive military training will rely on your basic skills to serve as foundation for everything else.

Give and Take

Serving your country in the military is one of the most selfless things you will ever do. Even if you serve a short time and never see conflict, you will always be a part of the American military family. In order to be successful, your time in the Army, like any relationship, must consist of give and take. If you "do" BCT the right way, you'll give much more than you take.

Your job is to leave BCT having given *everything*. Lay it all out on every task, on every range, on every Field Training Exercise (FTX), and on every Army Physical Fitness Test (APFT). Return to barracks each evening having given your best and nothing less. Only then will you be able to take something away, like pride, self esteem, faith in yourself, and the sense of accomplishment that you have earned.

That's how you do Army Basic Combat Training.

A Note to Older Privates

Using Your Age, Experience, and Training to
Your Benefit and the Army's

Overview

While the majority of new soldiers are between the ages of seventeen and twenty-two, many older men and women are joining the Army as well. I was thirty-eight years old when I started BCT and turned thirty-nine just before graduation, so I was the oldest soldier in my Company. I was also older than all of the cadre personnel, with the exception of my Battalion Commander.

The reason I bring this up is because I know some of you are thinking that you wouldn't be able to have someone younger ordering you around, telling you what to do. I thought about that too before joining, but I never gave it any thought while I was going through BCT. It never occurred to me that my Platoon DS was fifteen years younger than I was (at least not until I started writing this section of the book). We treated each other with due respect: the respect that he had earned and deserved as a Drill Sergeant and the respect that I had earned and deserved by wanting to become a soldier. Age differences never became a factor.

And the same went for the rest of the cadre. I acted like I was an adult who wanted to become a soldier, and they treated me accordingly. Oh, sure, they had their fun with me: calling me "Gramps," asking if I needed my food pureed before being served, reminding me to take my vitamins, and attributing my forgetting something to the early signs of dementia. Every once in a while, I was treated like I was seventeen, but only because I was making the same mistakes as the younger Privates. However, I also earned a few more privileges than most of the other soldiers, because I took on more responsibilities, accepted a leadership role, and proved (over time) to be trustworthy.

The one thing you'll want to be ahead on is your physical fitness. While being in good physical condition is important for soldiers of all ages, it can be more difficult for you as an older candidate to acclimate yourself to BCT if you've not been keeping a regular fitness regimen. In Appendix B, I outline and illustrate the Army Physical Fitness Test (APFT), provide basic physical training guidance, and give you pre-BCT APFT goals. Regardless of age, if you can meet those goals BCT will be much easier to negotiate.

Your Drill Sergeants really appreciate the older soldiers. I was told by several of the cadre personnel that it was motivating for them to see me out there, keeping up with—and in some areas, excelling past—the younger Privates.

> The younger Privates in my Platoon—and many in the Company— would come to me often and ask advice on a number of subjects. And why not? I was as old as some of their parents. I actually didn't mind, as I've always enjoyed problem-solving, so helping out with their dilemmas was second nature. Besides, I needed the practice for when my kids get older!

Turning Your Motivation, Experience, and Skills into Fulfillment, Money, and Rank

Just as the Army has many Military Occupational Specialties (MOS) that prepare soldiers for civilian life (we've all seen the commercials), civilians have skills, training, and experience that prepare them for Army life. Carpenters, engineers, electricians, mechanics, paramedics, nurses, police officers, etc. are all part of the Army family, too.

The Army is perfect for civilians who are unsatisfied with their current jobs or cannot find jobs doing what they were trained and schooled to do. It is also appealing to people like me who have satisfying civilian careers but want to contribute to their country and do something adventurous and patriotic, while keeping their civilian jobs (Reserve and National Guard soldiers). I am a full-time firefighter/paramedic, and I joined to use my civilian medical skills to benefit the wounded. Another soldier in my Platoon at BCT had an engineering degree and wanted to help rebuild war-ravaged cities, while another was a metropolitan police officer with a degree in criminal justice who wanted to become an MP (Military Police).

While I cannot speak specifically to each MOS and its particular equivalent training between the Army and civilian world, many are interchangeable, and some offer signing bonuses and the possibility of starting off with a little rank. Of course, the Montgomery G.I. Bill is still attractive to older soldiers, because it offers the chance to finish that college degree or to help pay off your college loans. And in the day when it's becoming harder to find a civilian career that offers benefits, the Army offers paid vacations; funded retirement; lifelong, comprehensive, individual and family health care; and a terrific tax-deferred savings plan (Thrift Savings Plan) that rivals similar civilian versions.

As you can see, there's a benefit to both you and Uncle Sam to use your age, experience, and skills in the Army. So don't let your age hold you back from going to BCT. It's more of a benefit than a detriment. Talk with your Recruiter to see what experiences and training will transfer to an Army MOS. You may be pleasantly surprised at what you find. Report to BCT open-minded, in good shape, and squared away, and it will all go smoothly; I guarantee it.

Table of Acronyms And Common Terminology

Recruitment-to-Graduation Flowchart

Acronyms

The Army acronyms I've barraged you with in just these first few pages are nothing compared to what you'll experience during your time in the military. Before we go any further, let's get a few of them out in the open early, so while you read, you'll have a point of reference and can get used to the Army acronym hell.

AAFES	Army Air Force Exchange Service
ACU	Army Combat Uniform
AIT	Advanced Individual Training
APFT	Army Physical Fitness Test
AR	Army Reserve
ASAP	As Soon As Possible
ASVAB	Armed Services Vocational Aptitude Battery
AWOL	Absent Without Leave
BCT	Basic Combat Training
BRM	Basic Rifle Marksmanship
CO	Commanding Officer
CONUS	Continental United States
DEP	Delayed Entry Program
DEERS	Defense Enrollment Eligibility Reporting System
DFAC	Dining Facility
DOD	Department of Defense
DS	Drill Sergeant
EOC-APFT	End-of-Cycle Army Physical Fitness Test
FTX	Field Training Exercise
ICE	In Case of Emergency
IET	Initial Entry Training
LES	Leave and Earnings Statement

MAC	Modern Army Combatives
MEPS	Military Entrance Processing Station
MOS	Military Occupational Specialty
MRE	Meal, Ready to Eat
MWR	Morale, Welfare, and Recreation
NCO	Non-Commissioned Officer
NCOIC	Non-Commissioned Officer in Charge
NG	National Guard
NLT	No Later Than
PCI	Pre-Combat Inspection
PG	Platoon Guide
PH	Personal Hygiene
POC	Point of Contact
PT	Physical Training
PX	Post Exchange
RA	Regular Army
RECBN	Reception Battalion
ROE	Rules of Engagement
SIT	Soldier in Training
SOP	Standard Operating Procedure
TMC	Troop Medical Clinic

Common Terminology

The Army has also taken the liberty of creating its very own vernacular, the likes of which make reading Dr. Seuss aloud seem tame. Knowing common Army terminology is a must, so here are a few to get you started.

AIT/"A"-School	The term "A"-School is old-school for what the Army now calls AIT, which is your MOS (job) training.
Basic/Basic Training	Shorthand for Basic Combat Training.
Baggage	"Issues" needing resolution, stemming from medical, legal, or personal problems, prior to becoming qualified to enlist.
Battle Buddy	A principle of teamwork in which a fellow soldier accompanies you everywhere during BCT, especially when addressing a member of the cadre. The Battle Buddy concept applies throughout your Army career.
"Bunk" or "Rack"	What the Army calls a bed.
Contraband	Anything that you're not supposed to have in your possession as a soldier-in-training. The most common items are candy, cigarettes, pornography, and weapons.
Cycle	Short for "Training Cycle." A cycle begins with your arrival at RECBN/BCT, encompasses all three training phases, and ends at graduation.
Detail	A short, temporary assignment or chore.
Fraternization	Inappropriate relations between soldiers of the opposite sex during BCT.
Go/No-Go	Army lingo for "pass" or "fail" and "yes" or "no."
Guidon	A small flag, usually associated with your Platoon or representing your Company or Battalion.

HOOAH! (Hoo-uh)	The universal Army motto, answer-equivalent to, "Yes, Drill Sergeant," and always said with great emphasis and enthusiasm.
Hooch	Army lingo for a pup-tent made from buttoning two rain ponchos together. There's no extra charge for the dirt floor.
Hoochmate	The poor sap who shares the hooch with you.
Leave	Army lingo for paid time off that you have earned.
Military Occupational Specialty (MOS)	Army lingo for "job" or "career."
Profile	Limitations placed on your work and training abilities as the result of an injury or medical diagnosis.
Range-Walk	Army lingo for speed-walking, just slower than a jog.
Reception	Shorthand for Reception Battalion.
Recycle	Being placed in another Company for failing to meet the graduation requirements during your original cycle.
Rucking	The Army version of the civilian recreation known as backpacking, only heavier and at a faster pace, without the shorts.
Smokings	Physical fitness sessions conducted as a form of punishment.
Split-Option Soldier	An enlistment option reserved for soldiers, usually incoming high school seniors, who must "split" their BCT and AIT training due to time constraints.
Squared Away	Disciplined, respectful, neat, and orderly.

Recruitment-to-Graduation Flowchart

To help you understand how the Army will move you through the process of becoming a soldier, I'm going to provide a flowchart (of sorts). While each phase has a chapter in the book dedicated to explaining the particulars in detail, this chart will hit the main points, showing you how you'll proceed from Recruitment to BCT graduation.

Phase	What to Expect	Purpose
Recruitment	⊕ Application processing ⊕ "1-1-1" fitness assessment ⊕ Background investigation ⊕ Waiver/exception submission ⊕ Discussion of MOS qualifications	The purpose of Recruitment is to answer questions, outline the benefits of becoming a soldier, begin the qualification process, take preliminary examinations, and guide you through the enlistment process.
Military Entrance and Processing Station (MEPS)	⊕ ASVAB ⊕ Physical ⊕ Career counseling ⊕ Choosing MOS ⊕ Enlistment contract signing ⊕ Ship-out to RECBN/BCT	The purpose of MEPS is to ensure that you meet all the necessary qualifications to join the U.S. Army. Here, you will also decide on an MOS, sign your enlistment contract, and ship out to Reception/BCT.

Future Soldier Function (FSF) or Recruit Sustainment Program (RSP)	✛ Preparation for BCT ✛ Physical fitness training ✛ Intro to basic soldiering ✛ Administrative housekeeping	Once you sign your enlistment contract with MEPS, you'll attend either FSF or RSP, depending on your component (RA, AR, or NG). Here, you'll get a head start on soldiering before you ship to Reception/BCT.
Reception Battalion (RECBN)	✛ Lasts seven to ten days ✛ Introduction to BCT ✛ In-processing (paperwork) ✛ Uniform issue ✛ Additional health screenings ✛ Pay, rank, and benefit confirmation ✛ Immunizations ✛ Ship-out to BCT company	RECBN is your first stop when you arrive at your BCT station. You'll stay here a short while before being assigned to a BCT Company. Your time will be spent receiving uniforms, finalizing your paperwork, receiving handbooks, ensuring that your pay and rank are correct, clearing up medical issues (optical, dental), and preparing you for life "down-range" at BCT.
Basic Combat Training (BCT)	✛ Nine Weeks ✛ Basic soldiering ✛ Primary weapon qualification ✛ Leadership ✛ Graduation qualification ✛ Ship-out to AIT or home	To teach you the basics and form the foundation as a United States soldier.

Recruitment

Selling the Army

Outside of your friends or family, your first brush with Army personnel will likely be an Army Recruiter. You've probably seen them in your high school, on college campuses, and at local career day events. They attend community functions, sponsor local recreation activities, and make their presence at high school sports events. You've likely received literature, promotional items, or videos in the mail as well.

They may even have called your house, sent you an e-mail, or personally stopped by. Then there're the billboards, television commercials, radio advertisements, magazine and newspaper inserts, and Internet promotions, complete with stimulating audio and visual effects.

Do you get the impression that someone is trying to sell you something? You should, because that's exactly what's happening. It's part of an organized advertising campaign aimed at sparking your interest in the armed services, the end result of which is to bring you into the sales office.

Lead from the Front

That brings us to the salespeople: Recruiters. Army Recruiters have one of the toughest jobs in the military, rivaled only by Drill Sergeants in regard to commitment, time, and energy spent on recruits. Nothing conveys the importance of the role of the Recruiter like the Army maxim, "Lead from the Front." The Recruiter is the face of the Army, and with good reason. Only soldiers who exceed performance and personal conduct standards can apply or be recruited (no pun intended) to serve as United States Army Recruiters.

Selling the Army is a rather daunting challenge. The Army brand isn't monolithic. Recruiters are tasked with finding qualified candidates and then selling them a whole new life, the heart and soul of which is the responsibility for the defense of life and liberty of three-hundred million Americans. There are no civilian careers that require the type of personal and professional commitment that the Army does.

"My Recruiter Lied to Me!"

Army recruitment tactics and techniques have been the subject of scrutiny for years, especially now, during times of war. The most infamous battle cry is, "My Recruiter lied to me!" For every one soldier who says that his Recruiter lied to him, you'll find a Recruiter who'll rebut this allegation by saying that they can't answer questions that aren't asked. The latter is generally more the rule than the exception. In other words, if you don't ask a question, they can't tell you the answer.

The confusion begins when prospective soldiers presume that their Recruiters will tell them every little detail of Army life, but it isn't going to happen. Your Recruiters will be spending their time, as they should, on important things to get you ready for life down-range and won't get mired in the minutia. If there's something specific you want to know about BCT or the Army in general, then you should ask or take it upon yourself to find the answer.

In the age of the Internet, you should be able to come into your Recruiter's office loaded for bear. Web sites, forums, blogs, and e-journals are just a few sources that make information about the Army instantly verifiable. Having said all of that, there is also plenty of misinformation in cyberspace, so you'll have to be careful where you get your sourcing. Stick with reputable Web sites, verifying any information you read with at least two more sources. If the fact checks out, then you can consider it credible.

The information available to you in cyberspace is incredible. www.goarmy.com, www.army.mil, www.usarmy.com, www.military.com, www.1800goguard.com, and www.armyreserve.army.mil are all reputable sites, chock-full of information. Keep in mind, though, that not every Web site will have up-to-date information on a particular Army component. For example, if you're looking for exclusive programs and incentives offered by the Army National Guard, you'll want to stick with their official Web site (www.1800goguard.com) for the most current information.

Do your homework, verify the information, print out your findings, and bring them to your Recruiter's office as a source of reference. With all the information that's available to you, there's no reason not to be able to ask more questions than they can answer on the spot. A good Recruiter (I had a great one) will always find you an answer to a question he doesn't know. Doing your homework proves that you're a serious candidate, and the Recruiter will likely treat you as such.

> *Like Drill Sergeants, Recruiters feed off of your energy. If you show up enthusiastic, they will be more likely to work harder for you. Just don't show up poker-faced. They aren't used car salesmen. Your browbeating won't get you a better deal. They can only offer you what the U.S. Army tells them they can offer, nothing more.*

Enlistment Timeline

There is no way to be specific about how long it will take you to enlist in the Army. The length of your experience, from the beginning of the recruitment process until you sign your enlistment contract, varies from one soldier to another and depends greatly on the amount of personal, legal, and medical baggage you walk in with. Once they become qualified, young soldiers with no baggage can process through within a few weeks and ship out shortly thereafter. Soldiers requiring approval of waivers and exceptions may take up to six months to process, depending on what the baggage is.

Regardless of where you land in all of this, you'll need to exercise patience with the process. The wheels of the Army will, at times, appear to be flattened. Maintain faith in your Recruiter to keep air in them.

Honesty Is the Only Policy

I'm not just talking about the Recruiter being honest with you; I'm talking about you being straight up with your Recruiter. The vast majority of failed recruitment attempts are the fault of the candidate, not the Recruiter. Uncle Sam wants you, but not if you're broken. In other words, unpaid traffic tickets, serious medical histories, criminal convictions, driving suspensions, current legal proceedings, debt collections, etc. can either delay or destroy your chances of signing your enlistment contract.

Your Recruiter can help you with some of these issues, but only if you're up-front at the beginning of the process. There's little a Recruiter can do to help you clear up an issue that you knowingly tried to conceal from the Army.

The only thing that soldiers hate more than the enemy is dishonesty, especially among fellow soldiers. I've seen a Recruiter made to look like a fool because his candidate's concealed past caught up with him the day before signing his enlistment contract. Honesty isn't just the best policy; it's the only policy, especially when it comes to getting your Recruiters to work hard for you. Make things difficult for them, and they will make things difficult for you.

Service, Beyond the Sale

If you purchased a new computer and you required service and support after the sale, would you expect to get help from your salesperson? They may offer limited assistance, but you're guaranteed to be referred to an 800 number for the rest. As a matter of fact, there aren't very many purchases that you will make in your life in which the salesperson will be a point of contact (POC) after the sale.

While Recruiters may be the salespeople of the Army, they offer service after the sale and beyond. This is the Army-equivalent of an extended warranty. Your Recruiter is now:

- ⊕ the first NCO in your chain of command (COC);
- ⊕ your advocate and agent during the enlistment process, serving your best interests while protecting the integrity of the Army;
- ⊕ a problem-solver, helping you through personal/financial/legal issues;
- ⊕ your representative at MEPS, ensuring a fair enlistment;

⊕ a point of contact (POC) for you and your family while you're going through BCT and AIT, in case problems or issues arise;

⊕ a fellow American soldier, a Battle Buddy, and a mentor.

In other words, your Recruiter has accepted the responsibility for honoring the Army's commitment to you, making sure that you are taken care of before and after your enlistment. If any issues or needs arise, such as help with filling out important paperwork like your direct deposit form, your Recruiter is the go-to person. He will even assist you with personal business, such as setting up a checking account with a bank like USAA. All you have to do is ask, which you should never be afraid to do.

Trust, but Verify

Your experience with Army recruitment, whether positive or negative, will most likely be a product of your own doing. Recruiters don't exist to lie to you or provide a means for a fraudulent enlistment. Their job is to place qualified candidates in service to their country. If you've done your homework, been up-front and honest, and you still don't think you're getting the straight scoop from a Recruiter, pay a visit to another recruiting station and get a second opinion. "Trust, but verify" is always a good rule to follow, especially before entering into any binding contract.

Like all goods for sale, somewhere within the commercials, advertisements, pitch, and pomp is the real product. While not everyone selling something can claim truth in advertising, the Army is generally spot-on. What you see is what you get, as long as you're willing to work hard for it, and there's nothing wrong with that.

The Military Entrance and Processing Station (MEPS)

Overview

The Military Entrance and Processing Station (MEPS) is your first glimpse into the military mind outside of your Recruiter's office. This is the place where you'll process the majority of your paperwork, take diagnostic exams, receive your medical evaluation (physical), agree on a career (MOS), sign your contract, take the "Oath of Enlistment" (swear in), and ship out to RECBN/BCT. Yeah, it's kind of an important place.

When you process through MEPS, you'll likely be required to stay the night before in the contract hotel. Your Recruiter will provide you with a ride to the hotel, where you'll stay two to a room and wake up early the next day for breakfast and a ride to MEPS. The reason they insist on the overnight stay is due to the early start time at MEPS (usually 0500 or shortly thereafter) and the history of candidates either showing up late or not showing up at all on their own. At the hotel, the Army has a captive audience and can make sure you're up-and-at-'em on time.

Your overnight bag will be inspected upon your arrival at MEPS. Contraband such as cigarettes, weapons, alcohol, and pornography will be confiscated prior to your placing your bag in a locker, so don't bring them to the hotel in the first place. I know what you're thinking: thanks for the advice, Mr. Obvious! There's a reason I feel the need to mention it.

On my ship day, a young lad decided to bring his unconsumed booze to MEPS, which of course they found on inspection. If he had been of legal drinking age, the booty would have been confiscated, and he would have received forty lashes (figuratively speaking). But he was only eighteen and ended up charged by police with Minor in Possession (MIP), barring him from further processing with the Army.

Wait; the story gets even better.

His two buddies whom he was partying and processing through MEPS with thought it was funny that he got busted and they didn't. However, they were in for a surprise, because part of the medical evaluation is a breathalyzer test. They both tested positive (legally intoxicated) and were barred from further processing as well.

As with the rest of the Army, there's plenty of "hurry up and wait" at MEPS. No matter what you're doing at MEPS, be prepared to spend the majority of the day there. Most MEPS (if not all of them) have a television to watch and some reading material. There is also a snack room and vending machines, and lunch is usually served in-house. You will not be allowed access to your cell phone or other portable, electronic devices during your time at MEPS.

Be sure to have your Recruiter's contact information (cell phone, office, pager, etc.) with you at MEPS, and bring with you a calling card or coins to use in the pay phone. (You can use the phone in the career counselors' office, but it doesn't lend itself to privacy, if needed.) Most of the time, your Recruiter will be with you while you're processing through MEPS, but at times, he'll be tending to other things. So, having a way to contact your Recruiter is a necessity if you have questions or concerns.

Armed Services Vocational Aptitude Battery Test (ASVAB)

Your first encounter with MEPS will likely be when you take your ASVAB test. The Armed Services Vocational Aptitude Battery is a computer-based exam that will determine the Military Occupational Specialty (MOS) that you qualify for. While you may have taken a pre-test at your Recruiter's office, this is the one that counts. The higher the score (categorically and overall), the more job choices you have.

I strongly suggest getting a study guide prior to taking the ASVAB. Your local library, bookseller, and the Internet offer numerous books and articles to suit your particular study habits. It's worth the small investment, not only for better career choices but also because a better or specialized job can mean a signing bonus and the possibility of a retention bonus when it comes to re-enlistment.

You're smarter than you think! *I've seen many bright and articulate soldiers who have had to accept certain MOS's rather than the ones they really wanted because they scored poorly on their ASVABs. Many of them would have made an MOS qualifying score if they had taken a little time to review and utilize an ASVAB study guide. One soldier in my RSP initially scored a twenty-eight, but with a little study time and some reference material, he retested and scored a sixty-nine. This was good enough to qualify for most MOS's, including, most importantly, the one he wanted.*

My point: you choose your MOS, don't let your MOS choose you!

Turn Your Head and Cough

Your next encounter with MEPS will likely be your medical evaluation (physical), where you'll spend the majority of the day on the medical floor receiving your screening. You'll have to disclose and document all of your health problems, if any, and explain scars, tattoos, broken bones, internal problems, allergies, etc.

Like I said before, this will be your first glimpse into military processing. You'll be told to "stand here, face this wall"; "sit in the brown chairs, facing the front counter"; "turn left out this door, turn right at the first hallway, and give your packet to the person in the second window." You get the point; it's all about following directions and paying attention to detail, just two of the many things that you'll be expected to do at BCT.

The Finishing Touches

Once your physical and ASVAB results are in and all other paperwork and documentation have been received, processed, and approved, your Recruiter will schedule you for another trip to MEPS to speak with a career counselor, choose an MOS, decide on a ship date, and sign your contract. By the time you reach this phase in the recruitment process, you should already have made a decision about which career field you will be going into or at least narrowed it down to a few choices. Your Recruiter will review your ASVAB results with you and discuss your goals, and you'll be given your MOS options.

With the advent of the Internet, there's Web site after Web site dedicated to providing information about the different MOS's. Just type the career name or MOS code into your favorite search engine, and you'll be inundated with information. In the chapter "Recruitment," I've included a list of reputable Web sites where you can find crucial information on the MOS of your choice.

Bon Voyage

Your final enlistment encounter with MEPS will be on ship day. Of course, you'll stay the night before in the hotel and be transported to MEPS the next morning to finish your out-processing. You may even swear in again (depending on what component you signed up for) prior to being transported to your mode of travel, usually before noon. In the chapter "Travel," I'll explain how you'll get from MEPS to RECBN/BCT.

Taking Care of Business

Overview

Before you ship, you should make certain that your personal affairs are taken care of, such as bills, direct payroll deposit of your military pay, legal paperwork, driver's license and vehicle registration renewal, etc. As a soldier at Basic Training, you'll not be allowed to pay bills, become involved in financial transactions, or participate in legal affairs or proceedings. With everything going on at BCT, you'll be lucky to have time to make a simple ATM withdrawal. In this chapter, we'll solve some common legal and financial problems and get you prepared to be personally less stressed at BCT.

Debts

Ideally, you should ship out debt-free. However, many young soldiers already have bills (credit cards, cell phones, car loans, etc.), so you'll need to make arrangements for them to be taken care of while you're gone. While you're a soldier at BCT, you'll not be allowed to write checks for bills or become involved in other financial transactions, with the exception of making ATM withdrawals from your bank account. For married soldiers, their spouses will most likely handle financial obligations, but for single soldiers, the best solution is to have your payments withdrawn electronically and automatically (auto-debit) from your checking account. Most creditors offer this option, and it's very easy to set up, so take advantage of the service. Later in the chapter, we'll discuss making your bank account easy to access and monitor while at BCT.

For those rare bills that cannot be paid electronically, you'll have to make the appropriate arrangements to have someone pay them while you're at training. Whoever it is that you trust to take care of this while you're gone, be SURE you can trust him or her to act appropriately in your stead. A family member is the best person to handle the obligation for most soldiers, but there are soldiers who do not have anyone in their families whom they can trust either. Depending on your relationship, your Recruiter may even be willing to assist you in sending off a payment or two from your account while you're away.

Either way, **DO NOT** ask a girlfriend or boyfriend or your drinking buddies to take care of things while you're gone. You wouldn't believe the horrors I personally witnessed with soldiers in just my Platoon alone who trusted friends or lovers to handle important things, only to find that they had no money left in their bank accounts or were getting threatening letters from creditors about bills not being paid. One soldier in my Platoon, who trusted his girlfriend to "handle" things while he was gone, completed BCT and AIT only to return home and find that his car had been repossessed, his bank account was drained, and his girlfriend was nowhere to be found.

In reality, regardless of marital status, you will only be able to rely on yourself to meet your financial obligations while away at training. The best solution for your debt is to eliminate it, but that's not always possible, so do the next best thing; contact your creditors and set up your bills as electronic auto-debits from your checking account.

> *Many of you, like me, have cell phones with contracts. My carrier (AT&T®) had a program that allowed me to place a "military hold" on my account until I returned from training. I faxed them a letter with a copy of my training orders, and they eliminated my payments for the months I was away and unable to use my phone. When I returned home, I called and had my service restored. It was that easy for me, and it's worth the call to your service provider to see if it has a similar program.*

Your License and Registration, Please

Before you ship out, take care of all legal issues and license renewals, such as driver's licenses, vehicle registrations, professional certifications, and any other legal paperwork that will expire while you're away. In the chapter "Recruitment," we talked about the need to be honest with your Recruiter about legal matters that need to be cleared up prior to shipping out to RECBN/BCT, and that should include any legal documents as well. If you're married, your spouse may be able to take care of some of these issues for you, but it's best to identify them and take care of them yourself before you leave for training.

The Buck Stops with You

Remember: signing up to serve in the military doesn't excuse you from your financial and legal obligations. Be sure to keep any receipts involved in satisfying all legal transactions, such as paying traffic tickets. In case of a dispute, a receipt or cancelled check is the proof you'll need to settle in your favor. No matter who handles your affairs while you're away, you are still ultimately responsible for the payments to be made and for the renewal of legal documents. It's in your best interest to handle all matters yourself without having to rely on someone to handle them while you're gone.

Making BCT a Financial Success

No, sorry; you're not going to get rich by going to Basic Training, but you can make most out of the money you earn at BCT by doing a few things before you ship. Here, I'll outline a strategy to help ensure that your money has a place to go, that it goes where it is supposed to, and that it is able to be accessed while you're having FUN playing soldier (I know I've said this before, but I'll say it again: it really is a lot of fun!)

Accessing Your Army Pay

Being able to access your Army pay while at BCT will require you to do three simple things: open a checking account, file an Army payroll direct deposit form, and obtain an ATM/debit card.

Your first step is to establish a checking account for your Army pay to be deposited into. If you already have a checking account, good; if you don't, open one at least one month before you ship to BCT and order an ATM/debit card (some banks assign a card automatically, without your having to request one). Even though you'll receive a book of checks with your account, you will not be able to use checks as a soldier-in-training. The ATM/debit card is your gateway to your cash.

There are two places where you can establish a checking account: a local bank and online. While a local bank may work for those who will be returning home after training, such as National Guard and Army Reserve soldiers, it will be a smidge inconvenient for Regular Army soldiers who are not stationed in their hometowns.

My suggestion to you, regardless of component and especially if you don't already have an established account, is to open a checking account with the United Services Automobile Association (USAA). The USAA is a financial and insurance organization designed specifically for military personnel and their dependents. Not only is this a service-member-friendly organization, but they make it "too easy" to handle and monitor your financial obligations while at BCT and beyond. They also provide:

- worldwide service to soldiers on overseas duty;
- investment services;
- free electronic bill-paying;
- great rates on automobile loans and mortgages;
- a full range of insurance services.

You can set up a checking account through them by going to www.usaa.com or by calling (800) 531-2265. There is normally a $25.00 deposit required (made by debit card) in order to open the account, but if you have recently enlisted and you ask nice enough, they may very well waive the deposit requirement. Your Recruiter will also be willing to help you set up an account with USAA or at least let you use his computer or phone to do it yourself. Just another service a Recruiter is glad to provide for a future soldier.

Once you've established a checking account, you'll need to file a payroll direct deposit form with the Army. This document will tell the Army to which bank and which account you want your pay deposited. Your Recruiter will provide you the form to fill out. You can complete it yourself or take it to your bank and have an account representative fill it out. At the very least, have a representative check over the form to ensure accuracy. After you ensure that the direct deposit form is married up to your checking account, return the completed direct deposit form to your Recruiter, but not before making a copy to keep for your personal records.

When you get your ATM/debit card, verify that it works *before* shipping out to RECBN/BCT. Using your ATM/debit card is the only way you'll be able to access your funds while at BCT, so verifying that it works before leaving is important. Your card will come with an assigned, four-digit code called a Personal Identification Number (PIN), which you'll enter on a keypad when you need to access your money. Don't forget to memorize your PIN. You'd be surprised by the number of soldiers who brought their cards but forgot their PIN numbers and couldn't access their funds.

> Ask your bank if you can customize your PIN to a four-digit number that you are familiar with and is therefore easier to remember than the one that the bank has assigned.

Now that you've verified that you'll be able to access your funds while at BCT, keep a modest amount of money in this account; around $200.00 will be enough. Why $200.00? Because your Army pay will be delayed for thirty days, and if it falls in the wrong spot during the payroll cycle, your pay may be delayed up to forty-five days before being deposited into your account! Just in case you're doing the math, this means your first pay may hit your account in the sixth week of the nine-week training program.

Even though you'll get a pay advance "Smart Card" at RECBN ($250.00 for males and $300.00 for females), that money can vanish pretty fast with your trips to the PX for essentials, like the seventy-five-dollar running shoes you'll have to buy. So that money you left in your account will be there for you to access with your ATM/debit card to use until your Army pay shows up.

In summary:

- ⊕ Open a checking account.
- ⊕ Apply for an ATM/debit card.
- ⊕ Match your Army direct deposit form with this account.
- ⊕ Activate the card and verify that it works prior to shipping out.

⊕   Leave some money in this account, because your Army pay will be
delayed thirty to forty-five days.

*Another wise thing to do is to bring a business card from your bank with
a representative's name and phone number on it, so you'll have a point
of contact in case you (or the Army) has questions about your bank
account. On the back of that card, write down your account number
along with the routing number (this is the number that specifically
identifies your bank for all electronic transactions, like direct payroll
deposit). Having this information while you are processing through
Reception is necessary to verify that the information is correct on
your direct deposit form.*

Spousal and Child Benefits and Housing Allowances

Another major factor affecting your finances will be the pay benefits you'll
receive if you are married, have children, or if you have a mortgage on
a home. As part of processing with your Recruiter and through MEPS,
your personnel file will include official copies of your government-issued
identification documents, like your driver's license, birth certificate, and
Social Security card. If you are married and/or divorced and have children,
your file will have official copies of their documents as well. Married soldiers
will need copies of their marriage licenses, and divorced soldiers will need
copies of their divorce decrees. If you hold a mortgage on your home, you
will need to provide the Army with documentation, such as a mortgage
statement.

By providing this information and having the Army verify it, you will
receive a stipend in addition to your base pay for having dependents and a
mortgage commitment. And pay isn't the only reason for the documents,
as they will also be used to qualify other important benefits, such as health
care for you and your dependents.

Your Recruiter will make sure to emphasize the need for you to bring
either the originals or official copies of these documents with you to
RECBN in addition to the ones held in your personnel file. Official copies
of these documents can be made through your Recruiter or MEPS upon

your request. If you opt to bring copies, make sure the originals are located where a family member or spouse can locate them easily, in case they are needed.

Like the need to bring an extra copy of your direct deposit form, having official copies of these documents acts as insurance in case the filed copies are misplaced.

"Go" or "Know-Go"

Know Before You Go

Once you sign your enlistment contract, your Recruiter should offer you the chance to attend training sessions designed to get you ahead of the game before you ship to RECBN/BCT. The Regular Army (RA) and Army Reserves (AR) have preparatory programs that are different than the Army National Guard (NG), but they're designed to accomplish the same objective: preparing you for a smooth transition through RECBN and success at BCT. How often and how long you attend this type of preparatory training depends on your "sign-to-ship" timeline. Delayed Entry Program (DEP) soldiers will have more extensive preparatory training than soldiers who ship out within thirty days of enlistment, who will be lucky to get in a few one-on-one sessions with their Recruiters.

The programs are also designed to ensure that your personal information is current and correct, clear up any new or unresolved issues, monitor changes in your health, and instill the need to maintain good personal conduct. Regardless of component, experiencing a little "Army life" before you ship, even if it's only a few hours a week or one weekend a month, is priceless. Plus, you'll interact with other soldiers, some of whom you'll be cycling with through Basic and beyond.

Future Soldier Function (FSF)

The Regular Army and Army Reserve currently have a training program called the "Future Soldier Function" (FSF). Soldiers in this program meet once a week and cover a number of topics, all of which prepare you for BCT.

Tasks include: twenty-four-hour military time conversion, drill and ceremony, marching, reciting the three General Orders, identifying Army rank structure, learning the Army Values, American military history, land navigation, and (of course) physical fitness training (PT). Your Recruiter will have a checklist, which he'll use to mark you a "go" or "no-go" (Army lingo for "pass" or "fail") for each task. Complete them all as a "go," and you'll earn a promotion to the next rank (PV1 to PV2).

Don't scoff. While a promotion in rank from PV1 Smith to PV2 Smith may still make you Private Smith, the promotion in base pay is about $300.00 more per month. If you have dependents or other allowances, it will be even more.

Recruit Sustainment Program (RSP)

The National Guard has a program called the "Recruit Sustainment Program" (RSP). The goal of the RSP is to prepare you physically, mentally, and administratively to ship to RECBN/BCT. Soldiers assigned to RSP will meet once a month, spending the better part of a weekend covering the same tasks as those soldiers attending FSF but with the benefit of experiencing a BCT-type environment. So not only will you learn about soldiering, you'll also do PT every morning, experience life in Army barracks, and eat at an Army chow hall. Your Sergeants will try to stress you a little bit, just enough to give you a taste of life during Basic.

RSP soldiers also have the opportunity to earn a promotion from PV1 to PV2 by demonstrating knowledge in basic soldiering and for passing the APFT. The program is called "Stripes for Skills" and requires you to be marked a "go" in all the categories in order to earn the rank and pay.

You'll also get paid for your time at RSP, even before you attend BCT! Not only will this add a few dollars to your pocket, it will ensure that your direct deposit paperwork is correct and that the pay from the Army makes it into the correct bank account.

If you are a split option soldier and you've graduated from BCT—in other words, there is a break in between your BCT and your Advanced Individual Training (AIT)—then you will attend RSP as part of your weekend-a-month commitment until you ship to AIT. Once you complete AIT, you'll most likely attend one last drill at RSP before reporting to your unit.

Go Before You Decide. Another option to consider before signing an enlistment contract is to ask a Recruiter about attending either FSF or RSP as a "Tag-Along." It will give you the opportunity to participate in Army training while experiencing a little of the Army way before committing to a contract.

Don't Be Just a "Go": Be a "Know-Go"

The more you know before you report to BCT, the easier and more enjoyable BCT will be for you. If your Recruiters offer the opportunity to attend training in addition to RSP and FSF, take them up on it. Take advantage of every opportunity for preparatory training that is offered and use the time spent with your fellow soldiers to build a learning relationship.

In the back of this book, Appendix A contains study material that is worth knowing before you leave for training. Even if you just spend a little time learning what you can, it will help you greatly during BCT. This information is also necessary to know if you're working on a promotion from PV1 to PV2 prior to shipping out. A pocket-sized "Know-Go Card" with all of this information is also available as a free download on my Web site: www.63daysandawakeup.com.

Travel

Wheels and Wings

MEPS will arrange your travel to RECBN/BCT. Even if you live five minutes outside the gates, there's going to be a ride provided. Everyone's mode of transportation will differ, depending on where you're traveling from and to. Some will ride buses, while others will fly. Most will have to do a little of both.

For example, once we finished out-processing at MEPS, we were taken by van to the airport, where we caught our mid-afternoon flight to Atlanta. At our rally point at the airport, we met up with other soldiers (about two-hundred and fifty) from other parts of the country who had arrived earlier in the day. Later that evening, we all loaded onto several motor coaches for the four-hour bus ride to Fort Jackson.

> The best thing you can do during your travel is rest. Our first "day" in the Army was forty hours long. We were woken up on Thursday morning at 0430, out-processed at MEPS until noon, flew out at 1530, arrived in Atlanta at 1800, left by bus at 2000, and arrived at Fort Jackson at midnight, where we were up all night and the following day in-processing until lights-out at 2000 Friday night.
>
> I did not take advantage of the chance to rest during travel, and I paid the price for it when I arrived at Reception. There's no telling what your first day will be like, so assume the worst. Sleep in the terminal and on the plane, bus, and van. You'll be better prepared for your arrival and "welcome" at Reception.

While out-processing at MEPS, you'll get an instruction sheet during your final briefing that will explain where to report, when they're expecting you, and whom to contact when you arrive at each particular travel hub. You will also be assigned a team leader (one of your traveling peers) who will be responsible for your paperwork making it from MEPS to Reception.

If you're traveling by air and your instruction sheet is lost, report to the United Services Organization (USO) office at your destination airport for further directions or to use the phone. Most major hubs have an office, and some are open late, especially when they're expecting an influx of GI's. If no USO office is available, contact MEPS or your recruiter.

Your Last Meal

You'll also receive a meal voucher "check" at MEPS, good for a preset dollar amount. During your final briefing, you will be told where to spend it and how to fill it out. We spent ours in the Atlanta airport, and all the food court restaurants accepted the vouchers, as they were used to the flow of soldiers to training. Our vouchers were good for dinner and several bottles of water for the bus trip. Whatever the amount, it can only be used at one place, so use it all.

What to Wear

Wear something comfortable and seasonal, yet appropriate for travel. Blue jeans, T-shirts, and running shoes are the norm, especially for soldiers shipping to warm-weather training stations. Jogging pants and sweatshirts are also acceptable, while shorts are not. Whatever you decide to wear should be clean, respectful, and in good repair.

You should avoid wearing novelty shirts in your travels. One soldier reported to Reception wearing a T-shirt with "I See Dumb People" printed on it. As you can imagine, his new Drill Sergeants took exception to the inference. By the time they were done with him, his shirt should have said "I See Angry People."

The most important article of clothing (believe it or not) is footwear, the reason being is that sometime within the first twenty-four hours, you will be issued your PT clothing, but you'll keep the shoes you wore. Not that you'll do much PT at Reception, but running shoes look much better with sweats than say, cowboy boots and loafers, which a couple of soldiers were stuck wearing with their PT uniforms for nearly a week before they were able to go to the PX and purchase running shoes.

Speaking of running shoes, don't go out and buy a new pair prior to reporting to RECBN. You'll be custom fitted and receive a "prescription" based on your foot type as part of your in-processing. You'll then be required to purchase new running shoes based on the fitting recommendation during your first trip to the PX.

To Bring, or Not to Bring:
That is the Question

What to Bring

Most training stations have Web sites with information for future soldiers, which will include a packing list of what you are to bring with you in your travels to RECBN/BCT. You should also be able to obtain a similar packing list from your Recruiter or MEPS.

While it is important to follow their lists specifically, I'm going to suggest items to bring in addition to what they require. From my experience and the experiences of other soldiers, having these little extras will make life easier for you at RECBN and BCT and take up little additional space in your travel bag.

- **White underwear and white socks (and white sports bras):** I've seen some packing lists that suggest only one or two extra pairs of underwear and socks. NO! Besides the PT uniform, you may not get all your issued clothing for three to four days, so you'd be stuck wearing the few that you brought for that time. So my suggestion, for males and females alike, is to pack a total of four pairs of both white underwear and white socks. In addition, females should bring one additional white sports bra. This will get you through to uniform issue, where you'll get your Army underwear, ACU socks, and ACU T-shirts, and up to your trip to the PX to buy more of what you need, such as toiletries and more white, PT socks. Females will also be given a shopping list prior to going to the PX for their required undergarments.

- **Foot and body powder:** A four-ounce bottle can last a long time at BCT and go a long way toward keeping rashes to a minimum. I powdered my feet at night and powdered my "friction points" (arms, shoulders, thighs) before training that required me to wear my ACU's, and I didn't suffer any rashes. The soldiers who suffered rashes were not powdering, and once they did, they did not have any problems. Bring a small, travel-sized bottle with you, and buy more as needed on your trips to the PX.

◈ **Wristwatch:** Another must-have is the ability to keep track of time. Many soldiers showed up without a watch and had to buy one at the PX. Our bay did not have a clock, so we were expected to synchronize our watches with base time. I purchased one specifically for BCT, and it was worn out by the time I graduated. Handy for fire guard shifts, FTX patrols, and necessary if chosen as leadership, as you'll not only be responsible for where your element is supposed to be but when they're supposed to be there. There's no need to spend big money on one; the main features you'll need are water-resistance, a back-lit display, and an alarm.

◈ **Black, spandex shorts:** These are an absolute must! Your Drill Sergeants will insist on your buying some while you're in BCT, but the PX never has any in stock. Bring a few pairs with you from home. Make sure they're black with no logo visible on the leg. These will come in handy to ward off heat rashes "south of the border," because the slick surface of the spandex creates a slide effect for your ACU's instead of direct contact and friction against your sweaty, salty skin. They are also great to wear during PT, because the issued shorts are a bit loose, and during certain exercises, your "stuff" will hang out. Need I say more?

◈ **Black, permanent magic marker:** You'll be able buy them at the PX, but it's a good idea to bring one so you can begin marking your issued uniforms, purchased clothing, and accessories as soon as you receive them. Be sure it is the broad-tip type, as you'll be coloring in stencils as well as marking your name. Before you ship out, it's a good idea to put your moniker on your civilian clothing and bag in an inconspicuous location as well.

◈ **Paper, pens, envelopes, and stamps:** While these items always seemed to be available at the PX, it doesn't hurt to bring a few of each with you from home. When you make your trip to the PX at RECBN, pick up enough to suit your communication style. Even if you don't plan on writing many letters, ink pens are a must-have for administrative paperwork during in-processing and note-taking during instruction. So always have plenty in your locker, and keep a few in the pen pocket on your ACU sleeve.

⊕ **Addresses, phone numbers, and phone cards:** In this age of everything being electronic, we hardly remember anyone's address and phone number, so put that technology to use; print off a list, and bring it with you. Also, pick up a phone card at your local mass merchandiser so you can use it to make your phone calls when allowed. Don't overbuy; 120 minutes lasted me all through BCT. Phone cards are also available for purchase at the PX if more minutes are needed.

⊕ **Copy of your direct deposit form:** In the chapter "Taking Care of Business," I asked you to make a copy of your direct deposit form before turning it in to your Recruiter to keep for your records. Bring the copy with you, and carry it during in-processing at RECBN, just in case something happens to the one your Recruiter filed. If you do need it, it's a lifesaver. If you don't need it, store it in your personal bag. Also, bring a business card of a representative from your bank, so you'll have a POC in case there's a mistake with your direct deposit form.

⊕ **Identification and official documents:** Your packing list will include the need to bring your driver's license or official, state-issued identification card. In addition to your I.D., you also need to bring official (certified) copies of your birth certificate and Social Security card. If you are married and/or divorced and/or have children, you will also need to bring copies of their documents, as well as an official copy of your marriage certificate or divorce decree. If your current spouse has had a prior divorce, you will need a copy of that decree as well. If you own a home, you will need an official copy of a mortgage statement. While official copies of these documents should be part of your personnel file traveling with you to RECBN, you should bring a few extra copies just in case. These documents are all necessary while in-processing at RECBN for the distribution of pay, stipends, and qualifying benefits. For further explanation, see the chapter "Taking Care of Business."

◈ **Prescription medicine:** If you are prescribed medicine for a health condition—one that the Army is aware of—then you should bring your medicine and a new, written prescription (with enough refills to get you through BCT and AIT) from your doctor. Your prescription will be filled after being verified by an Army physician.

◈ **Immunization certificate:** Bringing your shot record from your doctor might save you from a few of the seven vaccinations you'll receive while processing through RECBN. The document must be the original or an original copy and not a photocopy. See the chapter "Reception Battalion" for more details.

◈ **Money:** Your packing list will most likely include the need to bring cash (no more than $50) with you, but more important is the ability to access your money electronically through an ATM or debit card. Even though you'll get a pay advance "Smart Card" at Reception, you'll need a way to pay for the extraneous stuff, such as plaques and Platoon T-shirts, that you'll buy throughout your stay at BCT. Plus, you may need to buy extra, necessary items, which may exceed your pay advance. So bring one card that will give you access to an account, preferably one that your Army pay will be going into, so that you can access funds, check your balance, and verify deposits. See the chapter "Taking Care of Business" for more advice.

⊕   **Two (2) combination locks:** Your packing list will give you the option of combination or keyed locks. **DO NOT bring keyed locks.** Everyone in my Platoon who had a keyed lock eventually lost their keys and had to have their locks cut off. Buy a pair of same-combination locks, memorize the combination, and you'll be good to go through BCT. Why two locks? One is for your barracks locker, and the other will be used for your duffle when out on FTX.

⊕   **Cotton-tipped swabs (Q-tips):** Not only will you use these to swab dirt out of your ears and belly button, but you'll need these to clean the different components of your rifle. Don't buy the jumbo box. A travel-size will travel well, and more are available at the PX.

⊕   **Fingernail brush:** Frequent hand-washing is the single most effective way to prevent the spread of germs to others as well as to yourself. It does little good, however, to have clean hands and dirty fingernails. Bring a fingernail brush with you from home, and use it every evening during your shower.

⊕   **Sunscreen and lip balm:** A small, travel-sized bottle of sunscreen will go a long way to keep your skin from looking like a Texas rattlesnake. For the most part, your body will be covered by your uniform, but your face, neck, hands, and ears will be exposed to the sun and fry. So keep a thin layer of sunscreen on them. Your lips will also take a beating, so carry, use, and reapply frequently a lip balm with an SPF factor. More of each are available at the PX.

⊕   **Lint roller:** You won't need this until later in BCT, so you can either bring one or have one sent to you. Your class "A" uniform and beret will need to be rolled to remove lint and hairs prior to inspection and graduation. A small roller is all you'll need, so if one is available in a travel size, purchase that one.

As I stated earlier, this list isn't meant as a substitute for the packing list you received at MEPS or the one you downloaded from your training station Web site; it's meant to augment it. The little extras I'm suggesting will add to your comfort and adjustment to military life, so you can concentrate on better things like kicking some butt while you're at BCT!

No worries if you didn't bring a calendar, as you'll be able to count down the days in style every time you're out on range and use the portable toilet. The Portolet Picasso will never let you down, with the uncanny ability to pace off the remaining days of BCT. While the promiscuity of Mary Sue may be disputable, the countdown to graduation is usually right on the money. Most prior training cycles are on the same exercise and range table, so their countdown to graduation will be close to yours. So whether at BRM, the gas chamber, or on FTX, just let the outhouse artist keep the chronology!

What NOT to Bring

Just as your packing list has what to bring, it will also contain items not to bring, such as lighters, weapons, booze, or pornography. You will be allowed to bring and enjoy food during your travels, but you will need to dispose of it prior to the last travel segment before you arrive at RECBN. With new travel restrictions at airports, you may not be able to bring food and drink aboard aircrafts unless it was purchased beyond the security checkpoint. Just in case you were going to ask, leave the cigarettes at home. You can't smoke them at MEPS, in the airport, or on the bus.

Bringing portable electronics such as a cell phone, MP3 player, or other hand-held entertainment devices is also not advised. While these items will be stored in your personal bag for the duration of your training, a few soldiers found that theirs were damaged from the rough handling of their bags.

However, there is a benefit to having these comfort and communication devices when you have finished BCT and are in transit home or to your AIT destination. The best solution is to do what I did: pack a small, personal bag before you leave for BCT with a change of clothes, like your favorite jeans and shirt. In this bag, place the electronic devices (cell phone, MP3 player, etc.) you will want to have for your post-BCT travels. Leave the bag at home, and have a family member bring this bag with him or her when he or she comes for Family Day and/or graduation. This way, you'll have your goodies without the worry of them being broken or stolen.

Your Drill Sergeants

If I were to tell you on day one of BCT that the first person(s) you'd want to see and thank after graduation would be your Drill Sergeants, you'd probably call me a liar. But they will be.

The people (yes, they are human beings, despite what you've heard) who will lead you through every step of BCT and beyond will be your Drill Sergeants (DS). Even though you'll have specific DS's assigned to your Platoon and Company at BCT, *every* DS on the base is yours, and you are theirs.

It's a match made in heaven. Here's how it works. Their job is to train you, look after your welfare, help you both militarily and personally, mentor and counsel you, evaluate you, reevaluate you, instill discipline and administer punishment, and otherwise be one hundred percent responsible for you. Your job is to do exactly what they say, when they say it, and how they say to do it. It's really as simple as that.

A RECBN Drill Sergeant gives instruction to new soldiers.

These men and women are the best of the best. Only soldiers who exceed performance and personal conduct standards can apply or be recruited to serve as United States Army Drill Sergeants. Your DS's have the toughest jobs in the Army: take an undisciplined, untrained civilian, and turn him or her into a motivated American soldier. All you have to do in order to complete the transformation is exactly what they tell you to do when they tell you to do it. It's too easy.

It's Not Personal, It's Strictly Business

Whatever you do, don't take anything the Drill Sergeants say to you personally. Their business is to break you down to the core of your being and build you back up. Yeah, at times you're going to feel insulted, and sometimes it will sting. But there's an antidote, and it's called discipline: having the guts to dig down deep and change. So take whatever they throw at you with a grain of salt, remembering that it's being done for a purpose, and drive on. The process could be summed up in a number of ways, but I prefer to refer to it as your first real introduction to yourself.

You may feel as if they're working you too hard, not letting you sleep enough, and not giving you enough time to eat. But as you go through BCT, if you're being observant, you'll notice that when you're sitting in the shade, they're working in the sun. While you're under shelter, they're out in the rain. If you're up at 0400, they're up at 0300. And when you had five minutes to eat, they didn't eat at all. If that by itself isn't an indication of how dedicated they are to your training, I don't know what is.

Motivating Your Drill Sergeants. You'd be right if you thought that it was your Drill Sergeants' job to motivate you, but it's also your job to motivate them. A positive attitude, your outward enjoyment of the training, and a willingness to give 110 percent to each task is the fuel that feeds the DS's soul. It's give and take, a reciprocating role. Absorb their tutelage like a sponge, and squeeze it back at them every chance you get.

Role-playing

It won't take you long to see that your Drill Sergeants are expecting a lot out of you, but that's because your role and responsibilities as an American soldier demands that you be at your best, especially during times of war. Your fellow soldiers, the officers appointed over you, and three-hundred million Americans (and millions of liberty-seeking people around the world) are counting on you as if their lives depended on it, and they do.

The Humans Under the Hat

A Drill Sergeant instructs two soldiers as they negotiate the Individual Movement Technique (IMT) range.

At one time, your Drill Sergeants were exactly where you are now and many have been to war and back. They've all seen the results, and many have lived the sorrow and witnessed the deadly consequences of slipshod soldiering. Many times in war, there are no "do-overs" like you had when playing a game of kickball. They take their jobs personally, because they are personal. Give them the respect that's due and understand their most important role in your new life as an American soldier.

Greet them after graduation with a handshake and a hearty "HOOAH!" and then go out and do something GREAT with the training they gave you. They'll consider that payment in full for their efforts.

Can We Talk? *I'm going to let you in on a little secret: your Drill Sergeants go home every night and wonder if they're getting through to their soldiers. So prove to them that they did. After you graduate from AIT, drop your Drill Sergeants a line and let them know how you're doing and what's been going on with your life in the Army, and thank them for their time and effort. In those few, short sentences, you'll reaffirm to them that their endeavor was not in vain. They may not remember you, but that's not what's important. What matters is that you remembered them.*

Reception Battalion (RECBN)

Overview

Your second taste of the Army (actually the first BIG bite) will be your time at Reception Battalion (RECBN). Within ten seconds of your arrival, you'll know that you're not home anymore, and within the first twenty-four hours, you'll also understand why RECBN has earned the moniker "MEPS on Steroids."

Your Reception Battalion Drill Sergeants will "greet" you on the bus, rush you to off-load your luggage, and whisk you inside to start in-processing once again.

One of the first things you see as you arrive at the 120th AG RECBN, Fort Jackson, SC

"Shark Attack" is a term of endearment DS's use to describe the process of welcoming you at Reception and BCT. Before the bus driver has the chance to set the brakes, your DS will be aboard, asking you to kindly remove yourself from their bus. When you get outside to grab your bag, other DS's will be lined up to offer their assistance, telling you to slow down and walk, asking if they can help you with your bag, wondering if you enjoyed the trip and offering the opportunity to date their siblings.

You don't actually believe me, do you?

It's high stress and high speed, to say the least, but it's also short-lived and kind of fun, in a demented way. (It's all about attitude, right?) Just remember: keep swimming, little fishy!

The Method to the Madness

The reason behind RECBN is two-fold. One reason is to get your final paperwork processed (pay, benefits, rank, etc.), uniforms issued, immunizations, additional health screenings, ID cards, work books, and, of course, the haircut!! All of this is performed with as much speed and efficiency as can be expected when processing 250 soldiers at a time.

The other (and more important) reason is to be your introduction to the world of BCT: marching in formation, walking single file, chow hall etiquette, bay maintenance, locker and bunk standards, uniform and appearance standards, hygiene, and interacting/reacting with/to DS's, NCO's, and officers.

You'll be kept busy all day long, with plenty of "hurry up and wait" mixed in. But that's good; it gives you time to read the reference SMART books they issued you on the first day. Get used to spending your "down time" at both RECBN and BCT with your nose in these reference books. Carry them with you everywhere you go, and read them frequently. You will be quizzed and expected to know the contents.

Your time at Reception will be short, about seven to ten days, but you'll do a lot in that little time. While it may seem tedious, it's an important phase in making sure that you're ready for BCT. Pay attention here, and your days "down-range" at BCT will be easier.

Amnesty Room

One of the first stops upon arrival at RECBN will be the amnesty room. This is your one chance to anonymously surrender any and all contraband that you have in your possession without any repercussions. After this opportunity if you get caught with anything you're not supposed to have, you will suffer the consequences. In the chapter "BCT," I'll talk more about other amnesty opportunities.

Uniform Issue and Clothing Purchase

Of all the things you'll do at RECBN, receiving your uniform and accessories and purchasing other necessities will take a good portion of the time. The Army will provide you with the majority of your uniform needs with little, if any, out-of-pocket expenses for you. However, you will be required to purchase and maintain personal items to complete the uniform, such

New soldiers provide proof of receiving their issued uniforms and clothing during a "showdown" at RECBN.

as running shoes and white socks to complete the PT uniform. You will also be responsible for your other personal gear, such as towels, washcloths, laundry soap, toiletries, etc.

You'll be custom fitted for running shoes while at RECBN. You will be measured and have an impression made of your foot. You'll then receive a "prescription" and you'll use it during your first trip to the PX to select the proper running shoe for your foot type.

You'll receive a shopping list for whatever the Army doesn't issue, and you'll march down to the PX at RECBN and fill a basket with the requisite stuff. Part of the initial in-processing is to issue you a pay advance "Smart Card," which is similar to a debit card. The advance (males receive $250.00 and females receive $300.00) is deducted from your first Army paycheck. You'll use this card to purchase the necessities on your list when you make the trip to the PX. The amount the Army places on the card is more than enough to get you through the initial required purchases. Once the card runs out, you'll have to rely on your debit card or cash for whatever else you need or want.

Immunizations

The most unpleasant aspect of your time at RECBN is receiving your immunizations. You'll receive a total of seven vaccines during your initial in-processing and return for one more about halfway through BCT. The immunizations you'll receive are:

- ⊕   Tetanus and Diphtheria (TD);
- ⊕   Measles, Mumps, and Rubella (MMR);
- ⊕   Meningitis Conjugate (MGC);
- ⊕   Inactivated Polio Vaccine (IVP);
- ⊕   Tuberculosis skin test (PPD);
- ⊕   Influenza Vaccine (FLU);
- ⊕   Hepatitis B Vaccine (Hep. B).

The good news is that you've probably received some of these immunizations throughout your life. That means you can avoid some of these needle-sticks by bringing an original, up-to-date copy of your vaccination certificate from your pediatrician or physician's office when you report to RECBN.

Photocopies of your shot record will not be accepted, so ask your doctor for your original vaccination certificate. It's not a bad idea to leave a copy in your civilian medical file, just in case you misplace the original.

D.E.E.R.S.: Defense Enrollment Eligibility Reporting System

One of the more important in-processing stops while at RECBN will be with representatives at D.E.E.R.S., the Defense Enrollment Eligibility Reporting System. D.E.E.R.S. is a computerized database of soldiers and families who are entitled under the law to particular benefits, such as pay, stipends, health care, insurance, and retirement benefits.

New soldiers process through the D.E.E.R.S. office at RECBN.

Remember all that documentation your Recruiter and I asked you to bring in addition to what was supposed to be in your file? The D.E.E.R.S office is where it all gets entered into the system. As far as the Army is concerned, if it isn't in your file, you aren't entitled to the benefit, which is the reason for bringing the extra copies.

Battle Buddies

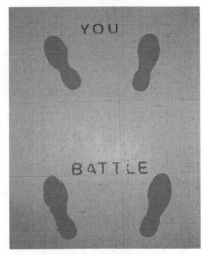

Here at Reception, you will also learn to do nearly everything in pairs called "Battle Buddies," a concept you will get to know intimately throughout BCT and beyond. Everywhere, and I mean *everywhere* you go, you and a fellow soldier will travel as a team. It doesn't have to be the same person (unless you're assigned a shadow or assigned as the shadow), but with few exceptions, it has to be someone of the same gender. It is especially important to have a Battle Buddy when addressing a DS or any other member of the cadre; otherwise, they will make short order of

A constant reminder to travel and address the cadre in pairs are footprints painted on the floor outside of the Drill Sergeants' office.

berating you in front of everyone within earshot before dismissing you as a nincompoop.

The Barracks Lawyer

Every Platoon has at least one and if you don't encounter them during Reception, they'll rear their ugly heads during BCT. The term "barracks lawyer" refers to fellow soldiers-in-training who, guided by their vast knowledge of nothing, presents himself or herself as the authority on everything. Listening to them and following their advice is a great way to find yourself in a heap of trouble. During my cycle, our barracks lawyer convinced a soldier that it would be okay to leave the Company area to make a phone call to their component representative. Guess who got in trouble? It wasn't the barracks lawyer. If you have a question, the only authority you should trust is your cadre. If it isn't heard from them, it should be regarded as bogus.

PVT Phone Home

You'll make your first phone call from Reception Battalion to let your family know that you made it there okay. You'll have a limited amount of time on the phone (usually about five minutes), so make it count. Choose a number that you know someone will be at when it's your time to call. Your DS will insist on your talking to someone or at least leaving a message.

Moment of Truth

Prior to moving down range from RECBN to BCT you will be given a period to claim anything that you have concealed from the Army, such as past medical conditions, prior legal problems, etc. The Army calls this opportunity the "Moment of Truth" and is your final chance to come forward with anything you need the Army to know about you. A few soldiers always step forward to admit to an allergy, or some other medical malady. By waiting for this period instead of claiming the matter during recruitment, these soldiers guarantee themselves the possibility of being held-over at RECBN to validate their claim. Full disclosure during the recruitment phase is the only way to go.

During the moment of truth there are inevitably a few soldiers who misinterpret this opportunity as a way out of the Army. One soldier in my Platoon claimed an allergy to dust. He was promptly told by a DS to keep his area dust-free before being dismissed back to the formation. The lame attempt not only earned him the nickname "Dusty", it also gave his Drill Sergeants a reason to expect him to keep his area extra clean at BCT.

Basic Combat Training (BCT)

It's All About Attitude

If you thought Reception was a rude awakening, you're about to step it up a notch. Your arrival at your Basic Combat Training (BCT) Company can be a reality check of the worst kind, especially if you're not ready for it (but YOU will be, because you're reading this book). You can do this, just as millions before you have.

I went into BCT expecting the worst, mentally and physically prepared for whatever they threw at me. My attitude was positive, and I kept my optimism. I was dedicated, motivated, and ready to do what they told me when they told me to do it. And simply because of my attitude, I didn't have one problem in BCT, and I'm no different from you.

The Secrets to Your Success

Later in this section, I'll discuss the different aspects of Basic Combat Training, but before we get to that, I want to give you the secrets to BCT success. If you heed my advice, I promise an easier and more enjoyable time at BCT (yeah, that's right, I said enjoyable; it really can be a lot of fun!)

1. **Grow up**. Sorry if that sounds rude, but it's your best bet to get the most out of your BCT experience. Act like an adult, get treated like an adult. Act like a child, get treated like a child. Too easy, right?

2. **Shut up**. Again, sorry for the harshness, but it's for your own good. It sounds like an easy thing to do, but this is where most soldiers get—and stay—in trouble. Keeping your mouth shut and your mind open is the path of least resistance through BCT. Otherwise, you'll be coughing up your Drill Sergeant's shoelaces every other day.

3. **Keep your hands to yourself**. BCT is not the time or place to expand your social registry. Nothing has brought about the demise of soldiers quite like fraternization, male and female alike.

(I'll talk more about this in "Crime and Punishment.") Keeping your mitts off others also includes grabbing, pushing, shoving, or other violent behavior towards your fellow soldiers.

4. **Do as you're told, and pay attention to detail.** Another way to smooth out your BCT experience is to simply do as you're told, when, how, and where you're told to do it. You will find salvation with your Drill Sergeants by following their orders as closely as possible. If you don't understand, clarify, then execute. Good soldiers clarify orders they do not understand, and good leaders appreciate your attention to detail and your willingness to do as instructed.

5. **Respect others and yourself.** Another way to draw negative attention to yourself is to have poor military posture (called "bearing") when in formation or when addressing a member of the cadre. Slouching, odd facial expressions, and "talking" with your hands are just a few of the bad habits you'll have to kick. A lack of military bearing shows a lack of respect for yourself and whomever you're addressing. Also, keep your eyes focused on an object directly in front of you, unless that object is the DS. In that case, focus on something behind them, and if they get directly in front of you, look "through" them, not at them (called "eyeballing").

6. **Stay awake.** Falling asleep at any time other than designated sleep time is a great way to draw the ire of your DS, not to mention that it's just plain disrespectful. If you feel yourself dozing off during training or classroom instruction, have the integrity to stand up and go to the back of the classroom, or just stand in place if out in the field. You might catch a little grief for it, but it'll be better than the alternative. Most of our "snoozers" were soldiers who stayed up after lights-out, talking and playing instead of resting.

7. **Be a good person.** Take care of your fellow soldiers, and help the ones who are struggling. Part of your job as a soldier is to make sure your Battle Buddies are squared away. If you see something that isn't right, help them make it right. Always look out for each other, and the same goes for looking out for your DS's. Without them, you'd be nothing, so if the opportunity presents itself to assist your cadre, be first in line.

8. **Have FUN.** Enjoying BCT is something you should strive for. By telling you to have fun, I'm not suggesting you take a haphazard approach to your training. I'm telling you that a positive attitude, some hustle, and a willingness to give 110 percent each day will make BCT more enjoyable for you, and that attitude will be contagious to your fellow SIT's and even your DS's.

If you can remember these eight simple secrets—*grow up; shut up; keep your hands to yourself; do as you're told, and pay attention to detail; respect others and yourself; stay awake; be a good person; have FUN*—you'll stand a better chance of enjoying BCT. Everyone who struggled during BCT violated these rules and paid the price in terms of punishment, extra detail, and the ire of the cadre.

A "Typical" Day

Each day at BCT is unique in its own way, and while each day may have a set schedule, changes occur frequently as necessity arises. Some things are fairly consistent, like wake-up, chow time, and lights out. Other times vary based on the tasks that are to be accomplished. This is especially true for night trainings. Here's a sample day for when you are in the barracks:

```
0430–0500: Wake-up, personal hygiene
0530: Lights on, DS arrival, inspection
0545: First formation
0600: Physical fitness training (PT)
0715: Chow
0800: Training
1200: Chow
1230: Training
1700: Chow
1730: Training, DS time, mail call, personal time, showers
2100: Head count, lights out
```

When out on FTX, your schedule will vary because of the activities associated with being in the field. Sleep deprivation is common on FTX, so if the opportunity arises during the day to catch a catnap, use the time to your advantage.

Physical Fitness

The biggest physical hurdle for you to overcome BEFORE reporting to BCT is becoming physically fit. I know what you're thinking (and it's the same thing many think before showing up to BCT): *the Army will get me into shape*. But due to training schedules packed with graduation-required tasks and skills that must be performed, PT will sometimes take a back burner.

Many in my Platoon and in our Company made the mistake of assuming that the Army would get them into shape and help them lose unwanted (and unneeded) weight. But this isn't the job of the Army. They came in overweight and in pathetic shape, and they suffered through BCT because of their apathy.

Drill Sergeant Lytle (far right) marches his soldiers back from
morning PT.

Prior to shipping to RECBN/BCT, your Recruiter is supposed to administer the "1-1-1 Physical Fitness Assessment," which consists of one minute of push-ups, one minute of sit-ups, and a one-mile run. The purpose of this assessment is to ensure that you're able to perform, to a standard, a minimum of thirteen push-ups, seventeen sit-ups, and a one-mile run of 8:30 or less for males and 10:30 or less for females. This obviously wasn't the case for everyone, as we had soldiers who couldn't perform even to these low standards on their initial assessment.

However, I want you to exceed these standards before you report to RECBN/BCT, because many tasks and drills during your training cycle, including road marches, rucking, confidence courses, team-building courses, obstacle courses, unarmed combat (MAC's), and even basic rifle marksmanship (BRM), require you to be physically fit in order to perform them with any degree of comfort and proficiency.

The Army Physical Fitness Test

The Army Physical Fitness Test (APFT) is the physical fitness assessment you will take throughout the course of BCT. You will take several of these assessments during your training cycle, most likely taking one at the beginning of your cycle, one at the end of Red Phase, and another at the end of White Phase. But the most important one is the End-of-Cycle APFT (EOC-APFT). This is the pass-or-fail "final exam." And just like your "finals" in school, everyone tries to cram for this test, too. To give you an idea of how seriously the Army takes it, you will not graduate from BCT without passing your EOC-APFT. Here, I'll briefly describe each event in the APFT. A comprehensive tutorial and illustrated guide to the components of the Army Physical Fitness Test is located in Appendix B.

The APFT consists of three different events designed to assess muscular strength, muscular endurance, and cardiovascular conditioning. Each exercise is either timed (push-ups and sit-ups) or designed to be performed within a certain time frame (two-mile run). Scoring of the push-ups and two-mile run are age-and gender-based. Sit-ups are scored the same regardless of gender but have allowances for age. Generally speaking, the younger you are, the more you're required to do and the faster you're required to run in order to pass. *A score of equal to or more than fifty points in each event is required to pass your BCT EOC-APFT.*

The push-up is the first exercise performed in the APFT. You will have two minutes to perform as many CORRECT push-ups as you can. You may stop, but there are restrictions on how you may rest in between repetitions.

The sit-up is the second exercise performed in the APFT. Like the push-up, you will have two minutes to perform as many CORRECT sit-ups as you can. You may stop, but there are restrictions on how you may rest in between repetitions.

The two-mile run is the final event in the APFT and is always performed after the push-ups and sit-ups. Your goal is to run two miles as fast as you can, but you must do it in less than the required time in order to pass.

There are charts available which break down each event into points based on age, gender, repetitions, and run time, but I will not be including them in the book, because exact individual event scores are not important for you to worry about yet. The goal I want you to set for yourself in each of the event categories prior to reporting to BCT, regardless of age, are the following:

	Push-ups	Sit-ups	Two-mile Run
Male	40	50	16:00 or under
Female	20	50	19:30 or under

These standards are the higher standards, based on twenty-seven-to thirty-one-year-olds, so regardless of age, meeting this goal will get you more than fifty points in each of the events, allowing you to concentrate on other aspects of your training. If you can achieve this and push yourself a little during BCT, you'll enjoy a natural increase in your scores due to the organized PT and "smokings," which is Army lingo for PT handed out as punishment.

So, think of the time prior to RECBN/BCT as a professional athlete would view the preseason: a time to get ready for the regular season. They wouldn't even think of playing the big game without a preparatory period, and neither should you. Reporting for BCT in poor physical condition will guarantee you nine weeks (and maybe more) of misery, discomfort, and unnecessary stress. The soldiers who struggled with their APFTs were the same soldiers who fell out of simple ruck marches, struggled with BRM, and performed poorly in other tactical exercises.

> *Appendix B contains an illustrated guide to the APFT, as well as basic physical fitness advice and training recommendations.*

Training Phases

BCT is divided into three training phases: Red Phase, White Phase, and Blue Phase. Each is significant in its own way, because advancing from one phase to another is an earned privilege, a sign that you and your Platoon are progressing as soldiers-in-training (SIT's).

There is usually a small ceremony to mark the passage by the Company First Sergeant (1SG), and the Platoon guidon (flag) will change to the corresponding color.

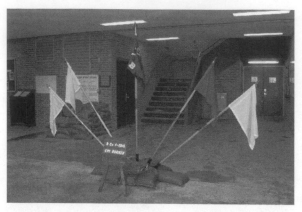

Colored guidons posted in the Company area signify the phase of each Platoon.

★ **Red Phase**

This is where you start. It's pretty much marked by total control, or "lockdown," by your Drill Sergeant. Your DS will be with you at all times during the day and evening. During Red Phase, you have no earned privileges, such as phone calls, extended personal time, or holiday routine. You will speak only when spoken to and engage another soldier in conversation only during training. In short, you have nothing unless it is given to you by your DS. Red Phase usually lasts only three weeks but may be extended based on behavior.

> *My Platoon was placed back on Red Phase after being in White Phase for two weeks because of behavioral problems with a few of our young soldiers. They couldn't control themselves and lacked the discipline to not act up in places like the dining facility (DFAC) and were caught arguing in formation. And being returned to Red Phase meant total control by the DS's, which meant lock-down. It was also embarrassing, because while all the other Platoons guidons were white, ours was back to red!*

★ **White Phase**

You have a little more control over yourself. Platoon Guides (PG's) will begin marching you to and from chow, and the PG will receive orders directly from the DS to have you execute in their stead. You may also have a little more personal time in the evenings (based on activity levels), which should be used wisely to conduct extended personal hygiene, clean uniforms and accessories, or square your barracks away.

On Sunday afternoons, you may be given additional personal time to perform locker maintenance, write letters home, study, or do additional PT. There's less direct supervision, and the cadre expect you to use your time wisely when organized training is not occurring. But with this new freedom comes responsibility, and you'll be punished for infractions (even more severely than you were during Red Phase), because you're supposed to know better.

★ Blue Phase

The final phase of training is Blue Phase. You'll enter this phase with the majority of the training investment behind you; now it's time to prove your worth. Your passage into this phase, usually between the completion of week six or seven, means you're expected to operate nearly autonomously, meaning as expected but without direct supervision. You'll also be expected to apply your knowledge and skills during a series of training events, some of which will be the most physically and mentally demanding of your training time.

> ### ★ *Black Phase.*
>
> *Hey, wait a minute; I thought there were only three training phases! Normally there are, unless your Platoon is a bunch of dunderheads, in which case the DS's will create a special training phase just for you.*
> *Welcome to Black Phase!*
> *A Platoon in our Battalion was placed on Black Phase, which consisted of total lockdown and smokings on the hour (night and day) for two days straight. Sounds delightful! Just another reason to stay motivated and square your Battle Buddies away.*

Your Chain of Command

During BCT, you will be introduced to the chain of command (COC). The COC is another military bedrock that you will be expected to understand and function within during your entire military career.

The COC starts with you and goes either up or down from there. As a Private (PV1), your COC is primarily up. But if you're an NCO (Corporal and above), your COC runs both up and down, as you're responsible for taking the orders from above, disseminating them through the soldiers in your charge, and then reporting back up through the COC to your superiors on the progress of the orders.

In BCT, your COC will start with your Drill Sergeants, particularly your Platoon Drill Sergeant. As a soldier-in-training, you'll be expected to know your COC all the way up to the Base Commander, usually a General. It is especially important to know the chain of command in your training Battalion, because that's your immediate COC if something goes wrong at BCT.

Following your chain of command is essential. Always give your Platoon Drill Sergeant the opportunity to answer your question or solve your problem before addressing the Non-Commissioned Officer in Charge (NCOIC) or the Company Commander.

Military Unit Organization

During BCT, you'll be assigned to a training Battalion, where you'll be divided into Squads, which are the elements that make up a Platoon within a Company. Confused yet? It's not really that hard to grasp. First, we'll break down the components—starting from smallest to biggest—that make up your training Battalion at BCT to see how all of the pieces fit together, and then I'll illustrate it with a map of a typical BCT Battalion.

★ Squad

At BCT, the Squad will be the smallest organizational element, usually consisting of ten to fifteen soldiers. You'll be assigned to one of four squads, which together make up your Platoon. A soldier from your Squad will be assigned as Squad Leader (SL), taking his or her position at the front of the element.

★ Platoon

A Platoon is the next step up from a Squad. A Platoon is generally made up of four Squads, usually consisting of a total of forty to sixty soldiers. A soldier will be assigned as the Platoon Guide (PG). His or her job is to assist the Drill Sergeants, taking a position in front of the Platoon. The Platoon Drill Sergeant is in charge of the Platoon.

★ Company

A Company consists of anywhere from two to eight Platoons, but at BCT, you'll generally have four Platoons assigned to each Company. Your Company will have a Commanding Officer (CO) and a Non-Commissioned Officer-In-Charge (NCOIC), along with other staff personnel.

★ Battalion

Your BCT Battalion will consist of anywhere from two to six training Companies. A Battalion is run by a senior commissioned officer such as a Lieutenant Colonel (LTC), and he or she will have a staff of commissioned officers as well as senior Non-Commissioned Officers (NCO's).

Here's a map which will give you a visual as to what your training Battalion might look like and how the different elements fit into the scheme:

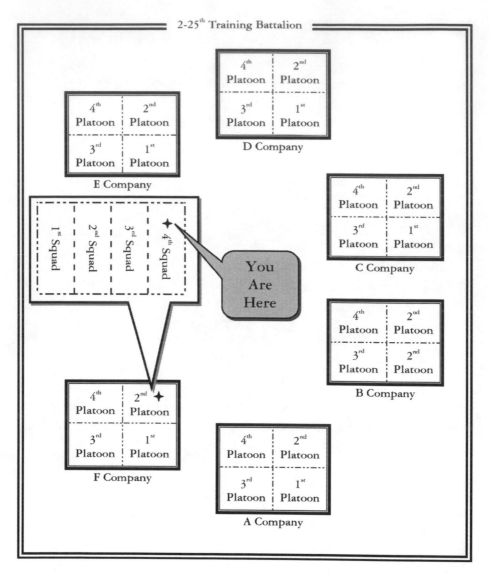

The ✦ represents you, as if you were assigned to the 2-25th Training Battalion, F Company, 2nd Platoon, 4th Squad. As you can see, the Squads make up the Platoon, the Platoons make up the Company, and the Companies make up the Battalion.

Soldier-Leadership

During your cycle, your DS cadre will choose the soldier-leadership for your Platoon. The leadership will consist of a Platoon Guide (PG), Assistant Platoon Guide (APG), and Squad Leaders (SL). These Privates are tasked with assisting the DS's in carrying out the daily routine.

★   **Platoon Guide (PG)**

This is the "ranking" soldier in the soldier-leadership position. At a certain point during BCT, the PG will take on the responsibility (as mandated by the DS) of troop accountability, disseminating orders, forming details, conducting drill and ceremony, marching the Platoon to chow, giving progress reports to the cadre, and preparing for the next day's activities.

★   **Assistant Platoon Guide (APG)**

This soldier helps the PG with his duties and is the go-to soldier for the Squad Leaders. The APG will act in the PG's stead.

★   **Squad Leader (SL)**

Most Platoons will have four Squads (also called Elements) with certain soldiers assigned to each Squad. A soldier will be assigned as the head of that Element and will be assigned as the SL. He may appoint an assistant to lead the Squad in his stead. The SL will report either to the PG or APG.

★   **Using the Soldier-Leader Chain of Command**

Whether a soldier or a soldier-leader, using the appropriate chain of command is essential to maintaining the continuity of the Platoon. Your soldier-leadership should always get the first chance at solving a problem before going to a DS. Your leadership was chosen for a reason, so give them the benefit of the doubt.

> *Your tenure as part of the Platoon leadership will usually be short-lived. The Drill Sergeants will want to rotate soldiers in and out of those positions to give the ones who show strength an opportunity to lead, if only for a brief period. So if you are looking for a challenge, keep yourself squared away, and you'll eventually find yourself in a leadership role.*
>
> *Don't let it go to your head if you are chosen. Leading soldiers is the most unselfish thing you'll ever do. It's all about them, not you. So be humble, put their welfare ahead of your own, and do what's right by them.*

Awards and Honors

The Army is a performance-based organization, and it likes to honor soldiers who possess exemplary skills and leadership traits. Your first opportunity at this award system will be during BCT, and the "interview" process starts on day one. Your cadre will be observing and will single out soldiers who exhibit leadership qualities and/or perform to a higher standard in tasks and drills. Not only will you be appointed to leadership positions, as we've already discussed, but you will be asked to study and compete for Company graduation honors.

★ Soldier Leader of the Cycle and Soldier of the Cycle

These soldiers exhibit leadership skills, excellent military bearing, exceptional personal conduct, and knowledge of basic soldiering. Soldiers who compete for these honors must appear before a review board made up of members of the Company cadre and answer questions consistent with the contents of their SMART books. They will also be expected to recite things like the Soldier's Creed, the Army Values, your General Orders, and other knowledge of basic soldiering.

★   High APFT Score and High BRM

You can earn other performance-based awards as well, which do not necessarily reflect your personal conduct but require exemplary performance in skills and tasks such as qualifying with your primary weapon and your EOC-APFT. Soldiers who score the highest in each of these categories are honored for their accomplishments.

It is possible to earn more than one honor, and I know of one soldier who was both Soldier Leader of the Cycle and High PT for his Company. As a recipient of one or more of these awards, you will be placed in a position of honor in front of your Company on graduation day, and your name and hometown will be announced over the PA system for all in attendance to hear.

Speaking of the Army

You've always said to yourself, "I'd like to learn a second language." Well, here's your chance, and it's going to be force-fed to you. The Army even provides the linguists free of charge (just another role the DS plays). Learning to speak *Militarese* isn't so bad; it just takes some practice and a few smokings for not saying "Drill Sergeant" at the beginning, middle, and end of every sentence, and you'll be fluent in no time!

Nerves interfere with sentence structure more than anything, not to mention that most of us are used to talking in a relaxed posture, using hand and facial gestures to help get our points across. In BCT, you'll be locked up in a modified position of attention, looking dead ahead, without any body language whatsoever. As with everything else new to you in BCT, this too shall pass, and by week two, you'll be speaking Militarese with ease. Now, if you could just get used to all those darn acronyms the Army uses, you'd be all set!

Shake-Downs

Whenever you move from one barracks to another, such as from Reception to BCT, you'll have all of your personal and Army clothing and gear checked for content. It's not necessarily a check for contraband as much as it is a way of making sure you've received and still have all your issued gear and clothing. During a shake-down (also called a "show-down"), all of your stuff is dumped out in front of you. A list of items will be called off, and you will find it and place it in the appropriate bag, all under the direct supervision of a DS.

So anything you have that's not allowed in your locker will be stored in your personal bag, contraband will be confiscated and disposed of, and the rest goes in your Army duffle.

Gettin' Smoked

"Front leaning rest position, move!" One of the least enjoyable aspects of BCT is what the Army calls "getting smoked." It's a term used for physical exercise given as punishment for an infraction, and there's *always* a reason to get smoked. This is especially true for the first half of BCT. Even if you're not the one causing the problem, you will pay for others' sins over and over again.

Push-ups, flutter kicks, overhead arm claps, jumping jacks (side straddle hops), duck walks, mountain climbers, bear crawls, and alligators are just a few of the DS favorites, and they come in groups of dozens at a time. Not doing them right? You'll get a one-on-one session with your new personal trainer: the DS!

Truth be told, smokings are the DS's way of getting in some extra PT as much as they are a form of punishment. I've been smoked first thing in the morning and last thing before bed, not to mention at first formation, in the chow line, during training time, before lunch, after lunch, after the evening brief, during personal time, after showers, and in the middle of the night because the fire guard shift was caught sleeping.

There's no way around them; smokings are a part of BCT life, so just get used to them. Remember: like many other things, they serve a purpose, so don't take them personally.

Chow

For the most part, depending on your training schedule, you will eat in the Dining Facility (DFAC). The food is served cafeteria-style, but with an Army twist. You'll have to get used to holding your tray in a particular manner and moving in a certain way through the chow hall. You'll also have to get used to eating very fast! Two to three minutes is all you'll have in the beginning, with an extra minute added later on. The speed at which the DS's have you eat isn't necessarily to be mean; it's to get you used to eating on the go.

It's also necessary to get you in and out quickly, as many other Platoons and Companies in your Battalion will be

Soldiers awaiting service in the DFAC.

following you, and seating in the DFAC is limited, so room has to be made for other SIT's. You'll also be limited in what you can and cannot eat. No worries: your DS will let you know!

> *We had to pay a "chow toll" for all meals eaten in the DFAC, and it was always paid in PT, such as twenty-five push-ups and sit-ups, before we headed back to the Company area.*

Meals in the field come in a variety of ways and are still expected to be eaten with a sense of urgency. Meals Ready to Eat (MRE's) are a field staple with wide menu choices, each complete with a snack, beverage, and accessory pack. It's a calorie-based meal, nutritionally balanced and meant for working soldiers expending energy. In the same vein as an MRE is a pre-packaged "brown bag" meal, known affectionately as a Jimmy Dean. At times, chow is brought out from the DFAC to the training site and served as what the Army calls a "Hot-A." The food is packed in insulated bins, served cafeteria-style, and usually complimented with fruit and juice.

> *Truth be told, the food in the Army is pretty darn good. No matter how, where, or when, you'll get three "hots" a day at BCT. At times, especially in the field, you'll be able to get seconds, as long as you're passing your APFT's!*

Barracks Life

Army living quarters are called Barracks. They vary in style from wide-open squad bays to dorm-room-style arrangements. Besides sleeping quarters, you'll also share showers, bathrooms, and attitudes with other soldiers.

Typical Army squad bay barracks. The desk to the right serves as the Fire Guard post.

★   Lockers and Storage

Each soldier will be assigned a wall locker upon assignment to his or her BCT Platoon. The wall lockers differ in shape and content. Some come with foot lockers or small cabinets with drawers, and others are wide open with shelves for organization of items. All have hanging bars for uniforms and gear. Whatever the design, you'll be expected to meet a locker standard, meaning that you'll have to organize the contents of your stuff to a diagram, and you'll be expected to maintain the organization and neatness throughout your stay.

> *There are never enough hangers provided for all your stuff at BCT. At your first chance, go to the PX and buy what you'll need plus six to eight more. Throughout your cycle, you'll be issued more gear that will need to be placed on hangers, such as your dress uniform and high-speed PT uniform.*

★   Sleep

In the Army, your bed is called a bunk, which, like Army flashlights, haven't changed a lot in sixty years. Most sleeping quarters are set up with bunk beds. Speaking of sleep, you'll get all the sleep you need, plus a little less. Actually, you're supposed to get at least four hours, but you'll get six to seven on a fairly consistent basis, unless you're pulling fire guard. Most nights, lights are out at 2100, and wake-up is around 0430.

One of the hardest adjustments for soldiers to make is the early but regular bedtime and wake-up that occurs in BCT. If you're currently a night-owl, it's a good idea to get yourself into diurnal habits before shipping out, even if it's not exactly the same time as the Army.

Some soldiers made use of a rare Sunday afternoon off to catch a catnap, and the Drill Sergeants would rarely say anything as long as the assignments and chores were done. Rest every opportunity you get; thirty minutes here and there can make all the difference in the world.

★   Personal Time

If any of you have seen the movie *"Stripes"* you may be under the impression that you'll get a weekend or two off, or receive an off-base pass while at BCT. The one word answer is; No. Besides the personal time allotted to you in the evenings and on the occasional Sunday afternoon, you will not be given any official time off or leave. No one was more disappointed in this fact than me as I was really looking forward to a mid-cycle mud wrestling exhibition. (If you want to know what I'm talking about, you'll have to watch *"Stripes"*.) Family Day is the only time in the cycle where you will be released on your own.

★   Personal Hygiene

Conducting personal hygiene (PH) is one of the most important parts of soldiering. There's an old saying in the Army: *If you don't take care of yourself, you won't be able to take care of anyone else.* Frequent handwashing, regular showers, and trimming nails are a few of the necessary components of good personal hygiene. Generally speaking, you'll have the chance and are expected to shower every day, with the exception of FTX.

Shower facilities vary from partitioned stalls to open-floor showers. I bring this up because many of you are shy or embarrassed about being naked in front of strangers. Not that that's a bad thing, but in the Army, it is a necessary evil. We had soldiers avoid showering until they were ripe, and that made for miserable life in the barracks for everyone, not to mention the ramifications of poor personal hygiene to your health. These same soldiers who avoided showering also suffered from health and skin conditions such as eye infections, stomach viruses, rashes, athlete's foot, and jock itch, which made life miserable for them. Yes, ladies, I'm talking to you too!

★   Sick Call

If you are suffering from an illness or minor injury and need to be evaluated by a medical professional, you will need to report to sick call.

Most of the time you will be evaluated and treated within the confines of the Battalion area by a medic, but other times (depending on the severity of the illness or injury) you will be referred to either the Troop Medical Clinic (TMC) or the base hospital. As with everything else at BCT, you will travel with a battle buddy to and from wherever you must go for treatment.

The opportunity to attend sick call is given first thing in the morning, Monday through Friday. For illnesses and minor injuries that occur throughout the course of the day or on weekends, you will most likely need to attend TMC for evaluation and treatment.

> **Sick Call Warriors.** *Basic Training is full of individuals who would rather spend their time at TMC than at BCT. Don't be a "Sick Call Warrior"! Use sick call only when necessary and be sure to follow the protocols of your Company when signing yourself out for medical care. Get better, and then get back to training!*

★ Conflict

Life with your new, soldier brothers and sisters is similar to life with your sibling brothers and sisters. It's impossible to not have some conflict when forty to sixty of you are sharing life in barracks. The best way to avoid unnecessary conflict is to be considerate of your fellow soldiers. Just because you want to be up after hours chatting and playing doesn't mean the soldiers next to you do too.

If there is a conflict with another soldier, it's best to talk it over with him or her first. If there isn't any satisfaction from that or it turns confrontational, approach a Drill Sergeant with a Battle Buddy and request an audience to air the grievance. Above all, remember that it isn't worth getting yourself jacked up with the Army by taking matters into your own hands. That's what your Drill Sergeants are there for.

> **Keeping it REAL.** *I'm not going to lie to you; some soldiers in your Platoon just won't get it. Despite intervention by the Drill Sergeants and senior staff, they'll still fail to comprehend the teamwork concept, will constantly put the screws to the entire Platoon, and will always be seeking conflict. In other words, they're inconsiderate pricks looking for a fight. I'm not endorsing violence, and after all, I just advised you in the previous paragraph to refrain from taking matters into your own hands. But sometimes, when all else fails, you'll just have to speak their language, if you know what I mean. That's just me: keeping it real.*

★ Fire Guard

Every night, you will have a fire guard roster assigned, the purpose of which is to get you used to pulling safety and security watch while your brothers and sisters sleep, just like you will on deployment. The schedule varies from base to base, but normally, two soldiers are assigned to one-hour shifts, starting at lights out and ending at wake-up. This task rotates through the bay, usually pairing up bunkmates. If your Platoon is assigned sixty soldiers and your fire guard shifts are one hour long, you will have to pull fire guard every third night or so.

Besides keeping watch, the fire guard soldiers are usually expected to perform chores while "on duty," such as mopping, cleaning the latrines, or doing laundry. Assigning soldiers to extra fire guard shifts as a form of punishment is another favorite of the Drill Sergeants.

Field Training Exercises (FTX)

One of the more difficult times (at least comfort-wise) will be your time spent in the field on FTX. During my time at BCT, we spent ten days (nine nights) on FTX when it was a hundred degrees during the day and rained nearly every night. Even with this, FTX can be very rewarding. It's all good, so just grin and bear it.

During the day, you'll spend your time on tactics and play war games, which are a lot of fun. The evenings are filled with more trainings, patrols, and tasks. Depending on the season, your tent (hooch) may consist of only two rain ponchos buttoned together to form a pup tent with a dirt floor. Performing personal hygiene (PH) while on FTX is challenging due to the limited, if any, places to perform the basics such as hand washing. Shortly, I'll give you some ideas on what you can bring and do to perform PH in the field as best you can.

At night, when you are out on FTX, you will be assigned to a patrol where you and another soldier will walk the perimeter of an encampment for the entire shift, weapons at the ready, challenging all who are found within or near your perimeter.

When you're preparing to go out on FTX, you'll be given a packing list by your DS, and your Platoon will pack its gear the same way and at the same time. A few of the items not included on that list that proved essential in the field are listed next. Most, like the hand-sanitizer, are available at the PX for purchase. Others are improvised from your already issued or available gear, and none are considered contraband.

- **MRE beverage bag:** This is the small, clear, plastic beverage bag found in your MRE pouch (NOT the green heater bag). Obtain one during chow and fill it with water in the morning, and set it next to your hooch out in the sun (in warm/hot weather) so that during the evening, you'll have warm water to use to conduct PH: shaving, bird-baths, etc. Your metal canteen cup will provide a nice little sink!

- **Washcloths:** Bring several with you (you can make them instead of having to buy them by cutting up an extra towel). Keep one in your cargo pocket, as there is always a shortage of napkins in the field.

- **Instant hand-sanitizer:** Another indispensable item is a four-ounce bottle of alcohol-based hand-sanitizer. Used only when necessary (before and after latrine and chow), it will last you a week in the field, not to mention that a dab on some TP will help sanitize the toilet seat. Keeping germs down to a minimum will help you avoid getting sick while out on FTX, where hygiene facilities are at a minimum.

- **Cordage (550 Cord or Paracord):** Within your Platoon, you'll likely have a large spool of small-diameter cord (thicker than a shoelace). Having a ten-foot length with you during FTX is another necessity to repair broken tent pole lines, stake loops, or lash your hooch down in case of a wind and rain storm. Just ask your DS for some, and it shouldn't be a problem.

- **Insect spray:** It may be on your packing list and it may not, so I'm listing it just in case. Even during the cooler months, you'll want to have some on hand. The non-aerosol kind is available at the PX, and a six-ounce bottle lasted my hoochmate and I for all our overnights in the field. Seven percent DEET as an active ingredient kept us bug-bite-free in the South Carolina summer.

- **Mirror:** At the PX, you will find shaving kits with small (business card-sized) plastic mirrors. If you are in need of a kit, buy this one and remove the mirror. Tape 550 cord (Paracord) to the back of it to make it look like a necklace (please, don't wear it like one!). This way, you'll be able to hang it up, allowing you to see your face to shave. If this shaving kit isn't available at the PX, buy the camouflage compact (face paint) instead. You may not use the paint, but the inside of the lid is a mirror.

- **Flashlight:** I know what you're thinking: well, duh! But it wasn't on our packing list, and some soldiers didn't bring one. Army flashlights (you know what they look like; they haven't changed in sixty years) are available at the PX. Be sure to bring and use the red lens filter, as you'll practice light discipline in the field. Also, buy and bring an extra pair of batteries, as you'll use your flashlight often on FTX.

⊕ **Sunscreen and lip balm:** These items are especially important out on the ranges and FTX, as shade is scarce. A travel-bottle-size sunscreen and the Army-issue lip balm will keep you from cooking, and both are available for purchase at the PX.

> Some soldiers swore by using body powder on ants to keep them out of their hooches. I did witness the powder kill the ants when sprinkled directly on them, and it did seem to work well for keeping them out by sprinkling the perimeter of the hooch with the powder. Another fine example of "improvise, overcome, and adapt." Just remember to save some for your skin!

Laundry

At our training station, we had an allotment taken out of each check for laundry and linen service. Each Tuesday, laundry was bagged and taken down to supply for delivery to post laundry, and each Thursday, soiled bed linen was exchanged for fresh. Laundry picked up on Tuesday was normally returned on Thursday, but it was occasionally delayed. While some might think of a laundry service as a luxury, in our case it was a necessity. Our in-house laundry facilities were inadequate for the number of soldiers needing to use them (our company had 240 soldiers and only four washers and dryers).

Your company may have adequate, in-house laundry facilities, in which case you'll do your laundry or combine loads with a buddy in shifts and on assigned days. Time will be set aside for this, but it may fall under your personal time allotment.

Creature Comforts

A little home-away-from-home can be a BIG boost to your morale. My "shrine" consisted of pictures of my wife and kids on the inside of my locker door, including a storybook written by my eight-year-old daughter (in case you're wondering, and even if you're not, it was called *The Best Soldier*). A small 4"x6" American flag hung gracefully from my top shelf and draped near my ACU's. My bible and the handmade rosary my wife made me were first in line for reading on my bookshelf. All of these small things added up to something BIG, and when things were tough in BCT, I could "go home," if only for a minute, remember why I was there, refocus, and drive on.

So bring a few, allowable creature comforts with you, such as pictures and religious items, and as you go through BCT, have other small, allowable things sent to you, such as letters and more pictures. Check with your DS before having anything other than ordinary correspondence sent to you.

Mail Call!

During personal time in the evenings, you'll be allowed to write letters. If you're like me, I wrote someone nearly every night, usually my wife and kids and occasionally my parents. This was primarily because receiving mail from family was a motivator and gave me something to look forward to each evening during mail call.

Remember: your being in BCT is stressful to your loved ones back home, too, as we often forget. So write to them often and reassure them that you're okay. It's even okay to admit to them that you're having fun! Ask them to write you often, even if it's just to say a quick hello and keep you up on the latest news, sports, or other interests. Besides letters and G-rated pictures, check with your DS's to find out what can and cannot be sent to you in the mail, such as magazines and newspaper articles. Photographs of a "suggestive" nature are prohibited.

Some soldiers in my Platoon wouldn't write home, because they were afraid that it would make them miss it more, and these were the soldiers who had the hardest time in BCT. Those of us who sent and received mail regularly were better-adjusted, because we had a good balance of military life and personal life, key to making the most out of your training.

Contacting You in an Emergency

Another more important reason to write home is so that family knows how to get a hold of you in case of emergency. If an emergency occurs (death in the family, disaster, grave illness, etc.) and you need to be notified and/or temporarily return home, your family will need to contact the American Red Cross to verify the emergency with them and to make the necessary arrangements.

Your family will need the following to make the notification and process the request:

- your unit number;
- your BCT mailing address;
- your Company Commander's name;
- your Social Security number.

The phone number for the American Red Cross is (800) 922-4469, or your family may contact its local chapter for assistance. In the back of this book, Appendix C contains a form for you to fill out when you arrive at your training Company and send to a family member, outlining how to contact you in case of an emergency.

> *Better yet, go to my Web site; www.63daysandawakeup.com, and download a free, printable, full-size version of this form. Since you will not know some of the information on the sheet before arriving at BCT, take it with you to complete and then send it home.*

Phone Calls

Unlike mail, which is consistent, phone calls are another matter all together. Depending on your Platoon Drill Sergeant, your phone call privileges may vary from once a week to once at the end of each phase of training (every three weeks).

At Reception, you'll make a phone call home, usually within the first twenty-four to seventy-two hours, to let someone know that you arrived safely, and technically, you'll get another one sometime after you arrive at BCT. But the others are dependent upon your command, Drill Sergeants, and YOU, meaning your and your Platoon's behavior.

Beyond the initial phone call, the others are earned privileges. While the Army cannot withhold your mail, they can (and will) restrict your phone calls. When you are allowed phone calls, they will last from five to ten minutes in duration and will usually be placed in the evenings.

Visitors

Before you ask your Drill Sergeant, the answer is NO; you will not be allowed any visitors while in BCT. Even if you and a friend signed up on the buddy system, your contact will be limited. One of the soldiers in my Platoon came into the Army with his brother, and they were allowed to see each other in church on Sundays only. The procedure for visitation may vary depending on your command and base, but this appears to be the rule rather than the exception.

> *The only exception to visitation I witnessed was that one of our soldiers got to visit with his father, who was a First Sergeant with a different training command on base. Even then, the visit was limited to ten minutes.*

Volunteering for Detail

The Army is an all-volunteer outfit, and if you thought the volunteering would be over once you joined, you were wrong. Throughout BCT, your Drill Sergeants will need soldiers for what the Army calls a "detail." Details are small, temporary assignments and can range from filling water coolers to filling trucks with gear and chow. Your Platoon will occasionally be assigned as the "Duty Platoon," which means you'll be assigned to provide manpower for special assignments throughout the day.

Either way, when the call comes, raise your hand or just run up and form up. Even if only a few soldiers are needed, everyone should make an effort to be part of the detail. It shows initiative, motivation, and enthusiasm. Rarely, and I mean rarely, are these details extremely laborious, and you'll usually complete them within an hour. Your DS's like to save the really ugly tasks for 1SG detail and other details assigned as punishments.

> *Sometimes, you get a reward for volunteering, such as fruit, a sports drink, or a snack. The best time to volunteer is for chow detail when you're out in the field. The detail consists of setting up the chow line and spooning out the portions of the Hot-"A" to the soldiers. While it is tedious, you'll be thanked in the end when you'll get to serve yourself, which means extra portions! Just eat it fast. You can (and will) taste it later.*

Keeping Your Things to Yourself

Believe it or not, not all soldiers-in-training (SIT's) are honest and trustworthy people such as yourself. Some are from troubled and checkered pasts and have histories of taking what isn't theirs. Things came up missing often during BCT, from simple, replaceable items like shampoo and ink pens to harder-to-replace items such as jewelry, money, and clothing. Always keep your locker shut and locked when you are not right in front of it, and don't give anyone the combination to your locker.

And it's not just the soldiers in your bay that you have to worry about. Soldiers from other Platoons frequented our bay in the evenings and on Sundays, and some were shady characters, steadily in trouble for one thing or another. Keep in mind the old *Godfather* saying: "Keep your friends close, but your enemies closer." Apply it during BCT. Make friends, establish some trust, but look out for yourself FIRST!

Sunday Worship Services

A variety of Sunday worship services are available at your training base, and a list of times and locations will either be posted in the barracks or available from your DS. You are free to attend the service of your choosing, and depending on where the service is located, you can either march or receive a ride there and back. Even if you're not particularly religious, attend a service each week. It will give you time to reflect on the week behind and ahead of you, and you may find a little spirituality and camaraderie to be another source of strength. Every little bit helps.

The Post Exchange (PX)

The Post Exchange is your new Wal-Mart! About every two weeks, you'll march there to get necessities (and that stellar haircut) and march right back to the company area.

Normally, the PX has what you need (toiletries, paper, pens, stamps, Ziplock bags, towels, socks, etc.), but it is occasionally out, especially of underwear and T-shirts. If you need to go to the PX for a necessity before your scheduled time, you'll have to arrange that with your DS, but you're better off borrowing from a Battle Buddy, if possible, until your next scheduled trip.

> On your trips to the PX, it's a good idea to buy extras of the toiletry items you'll use frequently throughout BCT. Bar soap, deodorant, toothpaste, and razor cartridges are all good to have an extra one or two of, keeping the chance of running out to a minimum. While the men won't require extra shampoo, a second bottle for you ladies is good to have on hand.

Your Personal Items

Contrary to the rumors and stories you may hear about BCT, your personal gear that you wore or brought will not be confiscated unless it is a prohibited item. All other personal items will be stored in your personal bag and locked up and returned to you just before graduation. The smart thing is to only bring the essential items and nothing more. You will not want to bring anything that is expensive or irreplaceable, such as heirloom jewelry.

I Wanna Go Home!!!!

So you want out? Here's a little food for thought before you decide to cross that bridge. I think it best to begin this section with a textbook example and a true story of why you shouldn't even consider it.

Private Partly Cloudy was in his first week of BCT and had decided after RECBN that he didn't want to be in the Army anymore. His strategy was simple: aim for a discharge for "failure to adjust to military life." He made up symptoms and would have little bouts of crying, seeking solitude, and fit-throwing. He was constantly going to sick call and forever on Profile, where he was prohibited from participating in training. In the mean time, his Platoon was steadily training and rolling along through all the mandatory events.

His time with our Platoon was particularly brutal, because he was not contributing to anything the other soldiers were required to do: cleaning, PT, fire guard, etc. At about week five, PVT Partly Cloudy received word that he was going home, and at the start of week six, he was reassigned to another training Company for further processing. He told everyone that he was heading for home at the beginning of week seven, but he was still in church on that Sunday, just as he was on the Sundays of weeks eight and nine. Word had it that he was still out-processing well past our graduation, with rumors that he was going to be recycled, not released.

So even if PVT Partly Cloudy was released at week seven, he would have only been two weeks shy of graduating and was done with the hardest part of BCT. So what sense did that make? Instead of spending his time at BCT fighting for himself, he spent his time and energy fighting the system. Like they'll tell you at Reception, the fastest way out of BCT is to graduate.

The negativity you feel during your initial days at BCT will change into something positive, guaranteed. Stay motivated, keep your focus, make a friend or two (guaranteed someone else feels like you do), and before you know it, you'll be walking tall, looking good, sounding off, and wearing your Class A's on graduation day.

Crime and Punishment

Getting in trouble during BCT is a great way to guarantee yourself a cycle of misery. I'm not talking about stealing or cheating, which will most assuredly lead you to legal proceedings, fines, and a possible recycle. I'm talking about kissing, hugging, and hoarding, otherwise known as fraternization and contraband.

★   Fraternization

Inappropriate relationships (you know what I'm talking about) between SIT's of the opposite sex is defined by the Army as fraternization, and it's one of the few mistakes you can make during BCT that can cost you in more than one way. While most of the time you'll be assigned extra duty (like First Sergeant detail) as a way to pay for the sin, you'll also be humiliated in front of the entire company.

Write a letter or pass a note to one another? The DS's will read them aloud, word for word, for all to hear. Get caught "together"? The DS who caught you will leave nothing to the imagination as he tells the entire company of your exploits. I have to say, it's one of the grimmest spectacles I have personally witnessed.

One male in our Platoon was caught with letters in the first week and was caught with other correspondence throughout BCT. Not only was he punished, but the females he was schmoozing also paid for the indiscretion.

So if the threat of reprimand and extra detail isn't enough to keep you straight, the verbal assault and humiliation should be. And if you're a female reading this, in each case of fraternization I know of, the male *always* had more than one "partner" at BCT, so you're sharing!

★   Contraband

Possessing prohibited merchandise such as cigarettes, candy, electronics, etc., is called contraband. The punishment varies from confiscation of the item to First Sergeant detail to having formal disciplinary action taken against the individual. Having food in the barracks is also considered contraband; just having the empty wrappers is all the DS needs to find you guilty.

The real problem with contraband is that everyone pays for the item when it's found, and it always seems to get found, no matter how well it is hidden. So everyone gets smoked, and the guilty party pays a little extra, if he or she owns up to it. If you really want to spend your time wisely, let the DS find contraband only to have no one admit to it. Now we're having FUN!

> *On the night before Family Day, the same night our personal bags were returned to us, we had a nice little smoking session at 0100 because someone in our bay was smoking in the latrine. Since no one admitted to it, we all got hammered for it. The DS finally got to the bottom of it, but not before we were soaked with sweat and scuffed up. And it turned out to be the usual suspects: the same little, insignificant turds who caused us trouble all cycle long.*

★   **First Sergeant Detail**

While there are different ways to be punished for infractions, one of the most popular is being placed on 1SG detail. Here, you'll have the privilege of performing laborious tasks in the evenings while everyone else has personal time. Assignments vary from janitorial work to useless, repetitive tasks like emptying and refilling sandbags. Regardless of the tasks, you'll be performing these on YOUR time, and YOUR time is very limited during BCT.

> *The fraternizing male in our bay spent the entire cycle on 1SG detail and only had personal time for a few Sunday afternoons. He lost all of his personal time for a few kisses and a candy bar, because he also got caught with contraband.*

★ Extra Fire Guard

Another popular punishment is assigning you to extra fire guard shifts, which can be the worst form of penalty because it interrupts your sleep, which you aren't getting enough of as it is. The infraction will determine the extent of your commitment, and it always seemed to be assigned to the miscreants on the night before a critical event, like qualifying with our M-16's. Somehow I don't believe that was merely coincidental.

Amnesty

During BCT, the Army offers you several periods to turn in any contraband you have in your possession without fear of reprisal. The first amnesty period is offered during your initial in-processing at Reception. This is the time to turn in anything you're not authorized to have during BCT or not allowed to store in your personal bag (weapons, drugs, alcohol, cigarettes, lighters, etc.).

Other amnesty periods are offered during BCT when you'll be allowed to turn in anything you've procured or concealed. There are also amnesty boxes available in your company area that can be used at any time to turn in anything you're not supposed to have or anything you've "found," if you get my drift.

> *Here's a clue: when the 1SG gathers the Company together and offers an amnesty period, and you have something, anything, that you're not supposed to have, turn it in or throw it away. A health and welfare inspection always took place shortly thereafter, and these inspections can be ugly; lockers get tossed, personal items are gone through, letters are read, and every nook and cranny of your bay is inspected for ill-gotten booty. While they're usually professional when going through your personal stuff (especially if they don't suspect you of having contraband), all it takes is for them to find something somewhere, and the gloves come off.*

The Final Week

The last week of BCT is a time of great anticipation for you and your fellow soldiers. It will be a busy time, as you'll be spending your days out-processing and packing your bags for your departure home or to AIT and your nights cleaning your gear and barracks for the next cycle. It all starts when you return from your final, week-long FTX (Victory Forge), culminates with a mid-week, final inspection by the Battalion Commander, and ends with graduation.

★ Family Day

Family Day generally happens the day before graduation and is the most looked-forward-to day of the cycle. You'll have the majority of the day to spend with your family members, and you'll be expected to return to the Company area at a certain time. We were "released" to our families at 0930 and had to report back at 1930, so we had ten hours to spend. There are a few stipulations, which may vary depending on command, such as whether or not you can travel off base, but the general rules prohibit alcohol and tobacco use and do not allow you to drive vehicles during the visit.

Most soldiers visit the base PX with their families and patronize the local food establishments. If you purchase anything, do not bring it back to the barracks. Remember: you're still considered a soldier-in-training. There will be a shakedown when you report back, and just as in the rest of the cycle, food and drink are not allowed in barracks and electronic devices will be tagged and bagged until after graduation. So eat your chow, drink your soda, and leave your goodies with family.

★ Graduation

This is what you've been working and waiting for. Graduation day is your last day of BCT, and it'll be over before you know it. We started the day early with a shower, an inspection of our dress uniforms, a final briefing from the Drill Sergeants, and a bus ride to the parade field. The graduation ceremony started at 0900 and was over by 1030. We were then bused back to the barracks to pick up our personnel files and our baggage.

Soldiers march to position on graduation day.

Split-option soldiers returning home with their families were released once they had their paperwork in hand. Soldiers traveling on to their AIT destinations were released as well, but with stipulations on when to return for their travels. Some soldiers were given permission to have family drive them to their AIT destinations, but it depended upon the location of the training site.

How long you'll have to spend with your family, how you'll get from BCT to AIT, when you'll have to return to ship out, what you'll be allowed to bring to AIT, and any other questions you have will be explained and answered during your out-processing in the final week. Of course, if you're attending AIT on the same base, some of these questions will already be answered.

Afterword:
The Quality of Courage

Courage is the first of human qualities, because it
guarantees all the others.

—Winston Churchill

Throughout the course of history, no one has exemplified courage quite like Winston Churchill. While he's probably no more than a blurb in modern history textbooks, Mr. Churchill led the free world against the Nazi war machine as prime minister of Great Britain during WWII. One of the greatest orators of all time, Churchill also knew that courage had value outside of war and would often speak to young adults about the necessity for personal resolve in everyday life.

The ravages of 1930s and 1940s Nazism was devastating and took the courage of an entire generation of free people to defeat. While the world has changed a lot since WWII, the devastating ideology of hatred is still alive and well. Your generation and the generations to follow will face an enemy every bit as dangerous and callous as its Nazi counterpart, and you'll do so without the benefit of confronting a uniformed army on a level playing field. This will require patience, adaptability, improvisation, and courage. That's where you come in.

The decision to wear the uniform of your nation is not one to be taken lightly. There's a reason that the ratio of soldier to civilians qualified to serve is 1:150. It means that soldiers are a special breed. There's something exceptional about Americans who understand the threat their country faces and are willing to place themselves in a position to do something about it. Every generation has had its heroes, and yours is no different. Each life given in the defense of freedom should serve as a reminder that none of us are Americans by accident and that citizenship has its purpose. Being willing to fight for the freedom of others while defending your own is your defining moment, providing the testament of a great national fabric, making us worthy to be called Americans.

Always negotiate life from a position of strength. Once you are defeated or quit, the ability to negotiate for your benefit and the benefit of others ends. Be a champion of freedom, and give your posterity the chance to do great things with it. In so doing, you'll prove to the world that good and free people did not bury their resolve with Churchill.

All that is required for evil to thrive is for good men to do nothing.

—Edmund Burke

Appendix A:
The Army Way

★ The Soldier's Creed

★ Warrior Ethos

★ General Orders

★ L.D.R.S.H.I.P.: The Seven
Army Values

★ Army Rank and
Insignia Chart

★ The Army Phonetic
Alphabet & Numerals

★ Military Time

Making a Good First Impression

Many young warriors ask what they can do to set themselves apart from the rest. One of the very few things you can do to impress the DS cadre is to be able to recite, with great confidence, the Soldier's Creed. So I am including it in my book, along with the four warrior ethos, your three General Orders, and the seven Army Values. I am including other need-to-knows as well to get you started on the road to the Army way. Read, memorize, and recite them, but above all, LIVE THEM.

The Soldier's Creed

I am an American Soldier.

I am a Warrior and a member of a team.

I serve the people of the United States and live the Army Values.

I will always place the mission first.

I will never accept defeat.

I will never quit.

I will never leave a fallen comrade.

I am disciplined, physically and mentally tough, trained, and proficient in my warrior tasks and drills.

I always maintain my arms, my equipment, and myself.

I am an expert, and I am a professional.

I stand ready to deploy, engage, and destroy the enemies of the United States of America in close combat.

I am a guardian of freedom and the American way of life.

I AM AN AMERICAN SOLDIER.

Warrior Ethos

A Warrior always places the mission first.
A Warrior never accepts defeat.
A Warrior never quits.
A Warrior never leaves a fallen comrade.

General Orders

1st General Order: I will guard everything within the limits of my post and quit my post only when properly relieved.

2nd General Order: I will obey my special orders and perform all my duties in a military manner.

3rd General Order: I will report violations of my special orders, emergencies, and anything not covered in my instructions to the commander of the relief.

L.D.R.S.H.I.P.—The Seven Army Values

Loyalty: bear true faith and allegiance to the U.S. Constitution, the Army, and other soldiers.

Duty: fulfill your obligations.

Respect: treat people as they should be treated.

Selfless Service: put the welfare of the nation, the Army, and your subordinates before your own.

Honor: live up to all the Army values.

Integrity: do what's right, legally and morally.

Personal Courage: face fear, danger, or adversity (physical or moral).

Enlisted Ranks

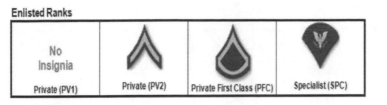

Private (PV1)	Private (PV2)	Private First Class (PFC)	Specialist (SPC)

Non-Commissioned Officer Ranks

Corporal (CPL)	Sergeant (SGT)	Staff Sergeant (SSG)	Sergeant First Class (SFC)	Master Sergeant (MSG)
First Sergeant (1SG)	Sergeant Major (SGM)	Command Sergeant Major (CSM)	Sergeant Major of the Army (SMA)	

Warrant Officer Ranks

Warrant Officer 1 (WO1)	Chief Warrant Officer 2 (CWO2)	Chief Warrant Officer 3 (CWO3)	Chief Warrant Officer 4 (CWO4)	Chief Warrant Officer 5 (CWO5)

Commissioned Officer Ranks

Second Lieutenant (2LT)	First Lieutenant (1LT)	Captain (CPT)	Major (MAJ)	Lieutenant Colonel (LTC)
Colonel (COL)	Brigadier General (BG)	Major General (MG)	Lieutenant General (LTG)	General (GEN)
General of the Army (GOA)				

Army Phonetic Alphabet & Numerals

A ALPHA	**B** BRAVO	**C** CHARLIE	**D** DELTA	**E** ECHO
F FOXTROT	**G** GOLF	**H** HOTEL	**I** INDIA	**J** JULIET
K KILO	**L** LIMA	**M** MIKE	**N** NOVEMBER	**O** OSCAR
P PAPA	**Q** QUEBEC	**R** ROMEO	**S** SIERRA	**T** TANGO
U UNIFORM	**V** VICTOR	**W** WHISKEY	**X** X-RAY	**Y** YANKEE
Z ZULU	**1** ONE	**2** TWO	**3** TREE	**4** FOW-ER
5 FIFE	**6** SIX	**7** SEVEN	**8** EIGHT	**9** NINER
0 ZERO				

Military Time

Learning to tell time military-style is another need-to-know. There are numerous ways to do the conversion in your head, but the best "study guide" is to buy a watch and set it to display in the twenty-four-hour military format (most name-brand digital watches have this feature). By doing the conversion in your head, telling time military-style will soon become second nature.

As you'll see in the table, the military drops the colon (:) between the hour and minutes. Time is always displayed and pronounced in the four-digit format, so 1:00 a.m. will always be written as 0100 and pronounced as "zero-one-hundred hours"; 1:06 a.m. will be written as 0106 (zero-one-zero-six hours); 10:49 a.m. is written as 1049 (ten-forty-nine hours); 6:37 p.m. is written as 1837 (eighteen-thirty-seven hours); and 12:15 a.m. is written as 0015 (zero-zero-fifteen hours). It gets a little confusing at midnight, which is written as 2400 (twenty-four hundred hours) until one minute after, where it converts to 0001 (zero-zero-zero-one hours).

Civilian Time	Military Conversion	Civilian Time	Military Conversion
12:00 a.m. (midnight)	2400	12:00 p.m. (noon)	1200
12:01 a.m.	0001	1:00 p.m.	1300
1:00 a.m.	0100	2:00 p.m.	1400
2:00 a.m.	0200	3:00 p.m.	1500
3:00 a.m.	0300	4:00 p.m.	1600
4:00 a.m.	0400	5:00 p.m.	1700
5:00 a.m.	0500	6:00 p.m.	1800
6:00 a.m.	0600	7:00 p.m.	1900
7:00 a.m.	0700	8:00 p.m.	2000
8:00 a.m.	0800	9:00 p.m.	2100
9:00 a.m.	0900	10:00 p.m.	2200
10:00 a.m.	1000	11:00 p.m.	2300
11:00 a.m.	1100		

Appendix B:
Getting In Army Shape

★ The Army Physical
Fitness Test (APFT)

★ Physical Fitness Training

I. The Army Physical Fitness Test (APFT)

The Army Physical Fitness Test (APFT) is the physical fitness assessment you will take throughout the course of BCT. You will take several of these assessments during your training cycle, most likely taking one at the beginning of your cycle, one at the end of Red Phase, and another at the end of White Phase. But the most important one is the End-of-Cycle APFT (EOC-APFT). This is the pass-or-fail "final exam." To give you an idea of how seriously the Army takes it, you will not graduate from BCT without passing your EOC-APFT.

The APFT consists of three different events designed to assess muscular strength, muscular endurance, and cardiovascular conditioning. Each exercise is either timed (push-ups and sit-ups) or designed to be performed within a certain time-frame (two-mile run). Scoring of the push-up and two-mile run is age-and gender-based. Sit-ups are scored the same regardless of gender but have allowances for age. Generally speaking, the younger you are, the more you're required to do and the faster you're required to run in order to pass. *A score of equal to or more than fifty points in each event is required to pass your BCT EOC-APFT.*

★ Perfect Practice Makes Perfect

Many of you have probably performed push-ups and sit-ups before, and many of you have done them in your own way, which may be the incorrect way, at least according to the Army. From now on, you'll practice doing them the Army way, because practicing like you'll play is the only way you'll improve your APFT score. We'll examine the push-up and the sit-up as a picture tutorial to get you tuned in for a stellar APFT score.

The Push-up

The push-up is the first exercise that you'll perform in the APFT. You'll have two minutes to perform as many correct push-ups as you can. You may rest during this time period, but there are only two authorized rest positions. You must maintain four points of contact (both hands and both feet) during the execution of the exercise, including the execution of either rest position. First, we'll examine how to perform a correct repetition, and then we'll examine how to execute the rest positions.

The starting position of the push-up is the front leaning rest, or "up" position. The arms should be fully extended with the hands in a comfortable position, fingers pointing forward, about shoulders-width apart. The body should form a general straight line from the base of the neck to the heels of the feet. The feet should be within six inches of each other.

The next movement is to lower the body, bending only the arms at the elbows, until the upper arms are just below parallel with the exercise surface. You don't have to touch the chest to the surface, but a good rule of thumb is to place a folded hand towel on the ground under your chest. When your chest touches the towel, you've gone down far enough.

The repetition is considered complete once you return to the front leaning rest, or "up" position. The scorer will then count this as a completed repetition. You only need to stop briefly in this position, just long enough to allow the scorer to judge it as a correct repetition, before continuing on.

Before executing one of the rest positions, you must complete the previous repetition by stopping briefly in the front leaning rest, or "up" position. Failure to do so will cause the last repetition to not be counted.

One of the two authorized rest positions is executed by keeping your arms and legs straight, but arching your back. You must maintain four points of contact (both hands and both feet) with the exercise surface while in any of the rest positions.

The other authorized rest position is executed by sagging in the middle. Your lower body is allowed to touch the exercise surface while in this rest position, but your arms must remain straight.

Upon completing the execution of a rest position, you must return to the front leaning rest, or "up" position before continuing your scoring attempt.

The Sit-up

The sit-up is the second exercise that you'll perform in the APFT. You'll have two minutes to perform as many correct sit-ups as you can. You may rest during this time period, but there is only one authorized rest position. As with the push-up, you must maintain proper form in order for the repetition to be counted.

The starting position of the sit-up is the "down" position, head and shoulders touching the exercise surface. The fingers are interlocked behind the head or neck and must remain so for the duration of the scoring attempt. The knees are bent so that the feet are flat on the exercise surface with an angle at the knee of approximately ninety degrees. The feet should be within six inches of each other. A spotter will hold your feet in position, bracing anywhere below the ankle using only his or her hands.

The next movement is to curl up the upper body, bending at the waist. Continue upward until the upper body breaks the vertical plane. Once this is done, you can return to the down position for the completion of a repetition.

The repetition is considered complete once you return to the "down" position. Unlike the start position, you need only to return the bottom of the shoulder blades to the exercise surface. The head and neck may remain off the surface. The scorer will then count this as a completed repetition. You only need to stop briefly in this position, just long enough to allow the scorer to judge it as a correct repetition, before continuing on.

The only authorized rest position is the "up" position. While in this position, your fingers must remain interlocked, and you may not use your elbows to "grab" your knees. Remember: once you finish resting, you must go to the "down" position for the repetition to be counted.

Two-Mile Run

The third and final event in the Army APFT is the two-mile run. The two-mile run is a timed event, meaning the faster you complete the course, the higher your score will be. Like scoring the push-ups, the two-mile run is age- and gender-based. During BCT, you'll run the course either on a track or on a flat road. You'll start the run as a group but be scored individually. You'll be assigned a specific scorer, to whom you'll be required to call out your name or assigned number each time you perform a lap. Running, or at least jogging, for the entire two miles is preferred over walking, which is allowed but highly discouraged.

★   Your Pre-BCT APFT Goals

I've said it before, and I'll say it here again; shipping out to BCT in good physical condition should be a primary goal. How much time you need to spend and what you need to focus on will depend on your current conditioning level. Before you ship to BCT, your APFT scores should be in the following range:

	Push-ups	Sit-ups	Two-mile Run
Male	40	50	16:00 or less
Female	20	50	19:30 or less

Being able to obtain these scores, regardless of age, prior to reporting for BCT will get you a passing score (and then some) in each of the categories. Don't make the same mistake that many soldiers make by expecting the Army to get you into shape during BCT. While the physical fitness applied by the Army during training will definitely help, organized PT will often take a back seat to other required training events, making it difficult for you to make the fitness gains you need. Prepare yourself before you ship, and enjoy the natural increase in your APFT scores due to PT, even if it is limited.

★   Testing Yourself

There's no need to run yourself through an APFT more than once a month. This will give you enough time in between assessments to judge the effectiveness of your PT routine. You'll notice that if you use the *Army Pocket Physical Training Guide*, it will suggest doing a different monthly assessment of your fitness level rather than the entire APFT. This guide uses the "1-1-1 Physical Fitness Assessment"; one minute of push-ups, one minute of sit-ups, and a one-mile run. This fitness assessment should sound familiar to you, because it's the same one your Recruiter will administer to you prior to shipping to BCT.

Which assessment you utilize is up to you. While the "1-1-1" is an effective assessment tool, remember: just because you can run one mile in eight minutes doesn't mean you can run two miles in sixteen minutes, and there's a big difference between performing one and two minutes of push-ups and sit-ups. In other words, there's something to be said for practicing like you'll play.

Whenever you decide to perform a fitness assessment, it's always a good idea to have someone else grade you, especially someone who will be fair in assessing correct form. Your Recruiter may also be willing to perform this assessment of you.

If you attend the Recruit Sustainment Program (RSP) or Future Soldier Function (FSF), you may perform the 1-1-1 Physical Fitness Assessment or the entire APFT each month as part of your PT requirement. This will save you from having to set up your own evaluation while providing feedback as to the effectiveness of your PT regimen.

II. Physical Fitness Training

The tasks you'll be required to perform as an American soldier will be physically demanding. Even if you are not assigned to an infantry unit, your primary responsibility, regardless of MOS, is that of a rifleman. This fact will be reaffirmed during your time at BCT, and you will be expected to be able to carry a standard combat load, including your weapon, on ruck marches that can total anywhere from five to fifteen kilometers (two to nine miles).

Since the demands are so great, the training you perform as a matter of readiness needs to be greater. The sooner you begin acclimating your body to the challenge, the better, and there's no time like the present. Some of you may already be well conditioned in one of these areas, such as running. If that's the case, work on becoming better at the others. The five areas we will concentrate on to get you there will be:

⊕ Calisthenics
⊕ Stretching
⊕ Running
⊕ Rucking
⊕ Nutrition and hydration

NOTE: Before beginning ANY exercise program, you should consult your doctor and obtain his/her approval or receive approval from the physician during the medical evaluation (physical) at MEPS.

In order to perform some of the exercises and components, you'll need to have access to some basics such as a pull-up bar, a running track/path, and a standard backpack.

★   **Calisthenics: Mastering Your Own Body Weight**

While having access to weight training equipment is nice, preparing for the rigors of BCT does not require an expensive gym membership or specialized equipment. Calisthenics (jumping jacks, mountain climbers, pull-ups, push-ups, etc.) is still the bedrock of the Army physical fitness training program. Your own body weight provides enough resistance to perform the exercises that are going to help you excel at BCT.

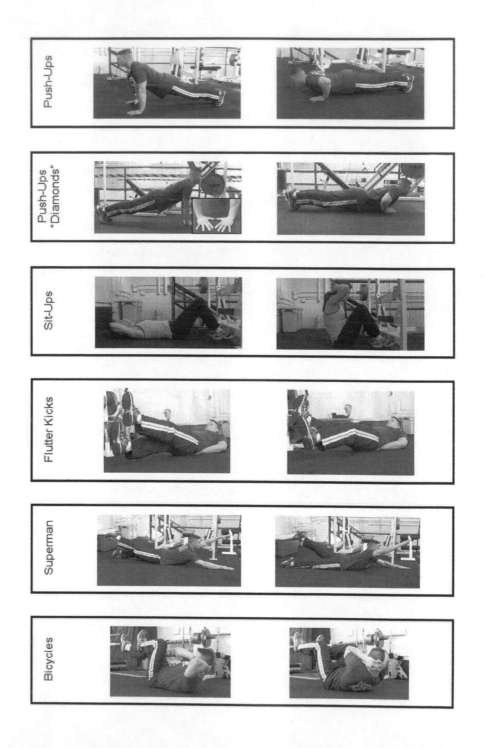

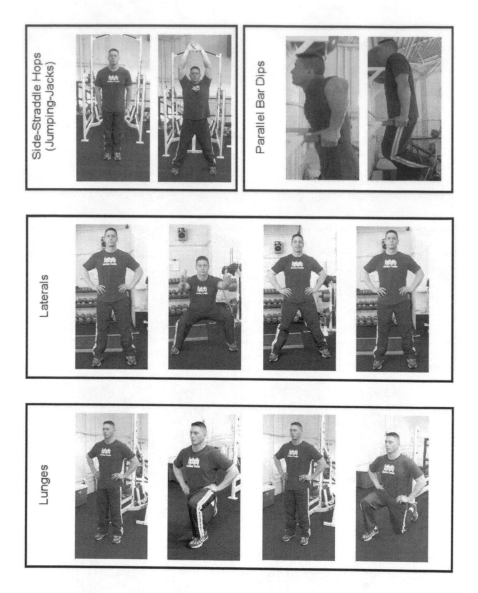

★   Stretching

Muscular flexibility is every bit as important as muscular strength. Tight muscles are more prone to cause discomfort, or result in injury, than flexible ones. With your regular regimen of strength and cardiovascular training, you should stretch before, during, and after your exercise session.

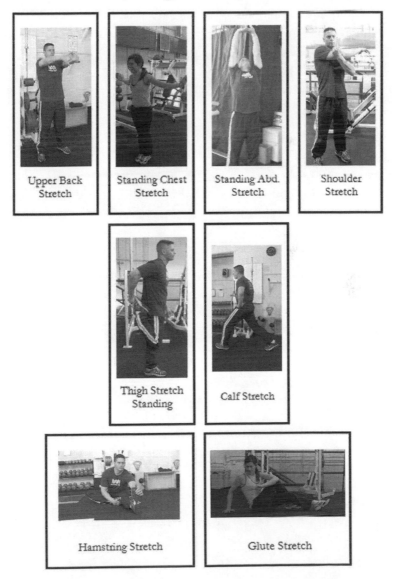

Upper Back Stretch	Standing Chest Stretch	Standing Abd. Stretch	Shoulder Stretch
Thigh Stretch Standing	Calf Stretch		
Hamstring Stretch	Glute Stretch		

★   Running

While the only way to improve at running is to run, some of you may not be in a condition to start there and may need to begin with walking. The best judge of where you should start is YOU, and there are many schools of thought on the best place to begin. A safe assessment to know where you should start is to run one mile on a flat, even surface, like a high school track. If you finish the run in 8:30 or less for males or 10:30 or less for females, then you can start with running.

If you failed this test, then you will have to start out speed-walking or slowly jogging and then eventually work up to a run. The amount of time it takes you to progress from one to the other will depend on your current level of conditioning. There's no substitute for just getting out there and hitting the road, but you should do so within your fitness level and progress at a safe pace. You'll be surprised by how fast the gains will come if you maintain consistency and try a little harder each time. Slow but sure wins the race.

Before you hit the road, hit the Web. *There are plenty of great running articles out there, and you're sure to find one that fits your style and current level of fitness. I did just that by visiting www. runnersworld.com before I shipped out, and I brought my two-mile time from 17:30 to 15:15 in a matter of four weeks by following some great advice I found on the site. The site also included short and long-distance training routines, and I was able to eventually run seven miles in just under sixty minutes. I wasn't going to break any land-speed records, but my fitness level was better than most at BCT, and yours can be, too!*

★   Rucking

Yeah, "rucking" is actually a word (at least in the Army). Rucking is the Army version of the civilian recreation known as backpacking. You've probably noticed that the Army has their own very unique styles of backpacks, which are called rucks, shorthand for rucksacks. As part of

A soldier wearing a standard ruck.

your pre-BCT fitness routine, I want you to get used to hiking with a backpack loaded with about fifteen pounds of stuff. In BCT, you'll ruck anywhere from five to ten miles, sometimes more, sometimes less, depending on the circumstances.

You don't need to go out and buy a special pack for this training, unless you don't have one and cannot borrow one. Most active people have a day-hiking pack, and most students have a book backpack, both of which will work just fine for this training. Load the pack with everyday items, such as old shoes and clothes. Placing a few concentrated, heavy items such as small weight-plates is fine, but they shouldn't weigh more than three or four pounds each. Again, you're looking for about fifteen to twenty pounds total. **Load the heavier items in the middle of the pack, close to your back.** Pad the area between the items and your back with an old shirt, if necessary, to keep an edge from digging into you while you ruck. Load the rest of the pack with your lighter, less dense stuff.

A hydration backpack is optimal, but if you don't have one, be sure to bring or have access to plenty of water for the trip. A good rule of thumb is to consume sixteen to thirty-two ounces (½ to one quart) of water per mile.

How you'll want to "wear" your load will depend on which type of backpack you have. If your backpack has a waist belt, you'll want to distribute the weight evenly between your shoulders and hips. You can do this by adjusting the load-distributing straps that come with your pack. As comfort dictates, you can move more of the weight either to the hips or shoulders by adjusting these straps or shifting the actual load in the pack compartment. Backpacks that only

When packed properly, a rucksack will be most comfortable with the load distributed evenly between the hips and shoulders.

Level terrain with easily distinguishable trails and a normal pace count make for the safest training.

have shoulder straps don't give you this option, requiring you to bear the burden over the shoulders.

Local parks with nature/hiking trails make the best places to ruck. They provide terrain features typical of what you'll encounter at BCT, and there are usually park employees around in case you need something.

Your pace shouldn't be any faster than a normal walk, which is about two to three miles per hour. Be sure of your footing, bring a trail map, and stay on marked paths. Let someone know where you'll be going, and take a cell phone with you, just in case. Dress appropriately for the weather, wear comfortable hiking shoes, and bring water and a snack.

Before you hit the trails, hit the Web. Your local, county, or state parks usually have maps of their trails online. Download and print off a map before you head out, so you'll know which park offers the best trails for your needs. Above all, have some fun while you're training. Involving a friend or a family member can make it more enjoyable and less like a chore.

★   Nutrition and Hydration

Your exercise routine will mean little to your body unless it has the proper fuel to perform the work, grow, and recover. At its core, nutrition is actually a simple concept and is easily applicable in everyday life. It's only when you're media-inundated on a daily basis with misinformation that the subject loses its simplicity. We're going to simplify the notion of healthy eating and talk about the most important factor: hydration.

No matter how hard you work at your physical fitness, the results will be limited without proper nutrition. In other words, **you are what you eat.** Nutrition does not have to be a complex topic, and good eating habits can be surprisingly easy to learn and do. Most of us know what is good for our bodies and what isn't. It doesn't take a rocket scientist to know that eating the cardiac-combo meal from your favorite greasy spoon and chasing it with the correlating bucket of cola is not a healthy choice. However, eating a deli sandwich and drinking water is. Without a diatribe on each nutrient component, a basic nutritional plan can be implemented with many of the foods you already enjoy. Here are some basic rules:

- Eat as many organic foods as you can (fruits, vegetables, whole grains).

- Drink water instead of refined sugar drinks like soda pop. The goal should be three to four liters of water per day.

- Consume lean meats.

- Avoid processed foods.

- Exchange refined sugar foods for healthful, naturally occurring sugar snacks like fruits and vegetables.

- Divide your large meals into smaller, more frequent meals.

- Don't eat during the three hours before bedtime.

- Avoid fried foods and abstain from fast foods.

- Prepare your meals yourself instead of getting take-out; this way, you'll know for sure what the ingredients are.

⊕ And for heavens sake, eat so that you can enjoy it, and don't be afraid to include some food that contains its own fat (meaning unprocessed, naturally occurring, *good* fats like in peanuts and milk).

> *This guidance is a good place to start on the road to eating better. For specific nutrient advice, food facts, and for meal plans involving all of the food groups, visit the United States Department of Agriculture's (USDA) Web-site at www.mypyramid.gov.*

Water is the primary nutrient, making up 70 percent of our body mass. Most nutrients and vitamins found in the foods we eat require water for proper absorption into body tissue, such as muscles. So it goes without saying that consuming adequate water is as important as consuming adequate foods. As a baseline, three to four liters of water should be consumed equally throughout the day. Additional water should be consumed during exercise or strenuous work at a rate of eight to sixteen ounces for every fifteen minutes of activity.

> *For some of you, counting calories may be of importance, as you'll be relying on calorie reduction combined with exercise to reduce significant body fat. If your plan involves a significant cut in calories or if your body mass has been defined as "obese," then you should consult your doctor as well as a nutritional professional, such as a registered dietician. For most, however, counting exact calories isn't as important as changing your eating mindset. Small, healthy changes in your diet combined with hydration, exercise, and adequate rest can be a powerfully positive combination.*

Dividing your large meals into smaller, more frequent meals is a great way to boost your metabolism while increasing your energy for exercise. This eating habit is common among body-builders and triathletes. Another benefit to eating like this is that you'll not get the sensation of being hungry, because every two to three hours, you're eating again. Skipping meals should never be done, as it causes irregularities with your metabolism.

Exercising right after a meal is not recommended. When you eat, blood is diverted to the gut for the digestion of food, which is why you feel sleepy after a meal. Hitting the exercise before your chow is digested is a great way to get an upset stomach and cramp up. Waiting sixty to ninety minutes after eating is a good rule of thumb. On the other hand, eating right after a workout is encouraged, as it provides the necessary depleted nutrients to open cells. A post-exercise meal balanced in carbohydrates (for restoration of energy) and protein (for recovery of muscle tissue), combined with plenty of water (for hydration and absorption of vitamins and nutrients), is the key to preparing your body for the next bout of exercise.

Weather and Climate Considerations

As someone who currently lives in a four-season climate, and as someone who has lived in a climate that features nine months of summer, I can attest to the need to modify where, when, and how you can safely train based on weather and surface conditions. The Michigan winter makes it very hard to be able to count on cleared, ice-free running paths, making access to a treadmill during these months a necessity. The South Carolina summer is equally as devastating to your training regimen, and accommodations have to be made for early-morning or late evening outside training to reduce the risk of heat injuries.

Regardless of climate in which you live, you will have to make accommodations for safe and effective training. The most important considerations are:

★   **Clothing and Exposure**

In cooler climates, dress in layers, so that they may be removed as needed and added back as necessary. Hotter climates require exposure consideration as well, such as sunscreen to avoid burning or a hat to provide some shade. Wearing the appropriate shoes for the activity you're doing is also important. Blistering up your feet by trudging in a pair of cruelly fitting shoes is going to put a damper on your training routine.

★   **Weather**

Knowing changes in the weather pattern when you're going out for a thirty-minute run isn't as important as knowing forecasted weather changes when heading out for a three-hour ruck. It goes along with planning your route to ensure shelter in case of severe weather.

★   **Hydration**

Consuming adequate water is just as important during activity in cool and moderate weather as it is during activity in hotter climates. Pre-hydrating yourself with twenty-four to thirty-two ounces of water thirty minutes prior to activity and then sipping down eight to sixteen ounces of water every fifteen minutes during activity is a good rule of thumb. Consuming a sports drink is also acceptable, as opposed to drinking only water. This is especially a good idea on warmer days, when the replenishment of electrolytes from sweating is necessary. Dilute half of the sports drink with water to reduce the nausea effect of the sugar.

★   **Access**

If your exercise plans are dependent on road, path, or trail conditions, you will want to consider their accessibility before heading out. Ice can appear in areas where snow has melted, and rain can cause washouts on trails, so keep the safety of your training route in mind.

Building Your Routine

The best way to train for BCT is to practice like you'll play. During your Basic Training cycle, PT will occur on most days except Sundays. Each day will involve flexibility drills and stretching, but the main exercise session will alternate between days of running and days of calisthenics. Rucking, while a muscular endurance exercise session in itself, is not a form of organized exercise; it's a mode of travel. So, you can occasionally expect to run three to five miles first thing in the morning or perform an intensive calisthenics routine and still have a multi-mile round-trip ruck march to perform in the same day. You should plan on spending time at least two to three days a week with your combat load on your back.

Knowing all of this, you should set up your training routine accordingly, allowing time for each component as your needs dictate. For as much as I'd like to, the task of prescribing individualized fitness routines based on everyone's personal needs would steer this book in a direction it was not intended to go. What I can do is suggest ways in which to perform the different components and then provide you with a sample week of training, in which you'll be able to adjust the intensity to suit your particular needs.

★ Calisthenics

A calisthenics routine is no different than any other fitness routine that utilizes resistance, meaning that the possibility of an injury due to over-training exists. There's something to be said for allowing your body a recovery period, which will cut down on the chances of injury. Taking this into account, two to three non-contiguous days of calisthenics per week is plenty and provides you with adequate rest and recovery.

The best way to prepare yourself for Army PT (and for the smokings you'll receive) is to perform calisthenics is in a circuit-training format, because that's how you'll perform them during BCT. Circuit-training involves several different exercises, each performed for a certain period of time before moving on to the next with no break in between. Here's a sample thirty-minute circuit-training routine.

One minute of push-ups
One minute of flutter kicks
One minute of pull-ups
One minute of crunches
One minute of mountain climbers
One minute of supermans
One minute of lunges
One minute of bench/chair dips
One minute of side-straddle hops (jumping jacks)
One minute of sit-ups
*** Repeat three Times ***

You'll notice that the two components of the APFT (push-ups and sit-ups) are in this example, and you should always include them when planning your calisthenics training. Switch up the other exercises you perform and add different ones each time you do the circuit. Work your way up to performing forty-five minutes of continuous calisthenics two to three times per week.

If extra attention to the APFT components is necessary, add a concentrated circuit of them, performing one minute of each for four sets once or twice per week. It can be done on the same day as another training event, such as a run or ruck. You can also perform them informally, such as knocking out a certain number of each during the commercial breaks from your favorite TV show.

★   Stretching

A good flexibility routine should be performed every day. On days when you're exercising (calisthenics, running, and/or rucking), you should perform stretching before and after your exercise session. On days when you are resting, you should still stretch twice during the day. A good stretching routine doesn't take much time and can be done any time you have a few spare minutes. It should, however, never be done when you are cold, such as right after you wake up. Get up and move around a little to get the blood flowing before you stretch out.

The eight outlined stretching exercises should be held for twenty to thirty seconds on each side and should be performed slowly with gradual, pain-free progression. This is called a static stretch and is the safest form of flexibility training. You may already have a stretching routine that you perform due to a sport you play, which may involve different stretching routines. Those are all fine to do, and the only thing I want you to do is work within your comfort zone so that you can avoid injury.

★   Running

Your running routine will be determined by your particular needs. While it's important to run long enough and fast enough to pass your APFT, two miles isn't the farthest you'll be required to run at BCT. It isn't uncommon to occasionally run from three to five miles during PT. While the pace of this run will be slower than what you'll do during your APFT, it will still require the stamina to at least jog for the requisite distance. For most, devoting two to three days a week to running, or at least jogging, is going to get you the best result. Like calisthenics, it's possible to run too frequently, which can result in an over-training effect on your run progression. The weather and season will determine when and where you will have to do your run training. Treadmill training can be as beneficial as road running. Improvise, overcome, and adapt.

Varying the intensity of the run is also important and a great way to improve your time. One of these methods is called speed interval training, where you alternate between sprinting for a certain distance or time and jogging for a similar distance or time. An example would be alternating sprinting for one minute and then jogging for two minutes, performing six sets for a total time of eighteen minutes. The same principle can be applied using a specific distance, such as sprinting/running for ¼ mile, then jogging for ¼ mile, repeating this sequence four times for a total of two miles.

★   Rucking

Spending some time under a loaded backpack will make life easier for you during your training cycle. Even people in great physical shape had to adjust to wearing a rucksack during BCT. Rucking is one of those exercises that reminds you of all those little muscles that you didn't know you had until you wake up the next morning after a five-mile ruck through sand.

So the sooner you get used to wearing a load for even short distances, the better and more comfortable the adjustment will be to Army rucksacks. Start out slow: one to two miles at first for inexperienced hikers and three to four for experienced, and then work your way up from there. Maintain a normal walking pace of about two to three miles per hour.

★   Utilizing the F.I.T.T. Principle

There's a common application theory when setting up an exercise routine called the F.I.T.T. Principle. F.I.T.T. stands for frequency, intensity, time, and type. When setting up an exercise routine, you'll apply each of these components in the following way:

⊕ **Frequency:** how often you perform the exercise session (every other day, twice per week, etc.).

⊕ **Intensity:** how hard you work during the exercise session.

⊕ **Time:** how long you perform the exercise.

⊕ **Type:** the kind of exercise you perform (cardio, strength, flexibility, etc.).

As a general rule, when intensity increases, your time spent doing the exercise will decrease, and the frequency with which you exercise will be determined by the type of exercises you perform.

★   A Sample Week

This is just a sample week's worth of training, and it can be customized to fit your needs and your current level of fitness. This example utilizes the F.I.T.T principle and takes into account a future soldier who is in good health and in good physical condition.

	Monday	Tuesday	Wednesday	Thursday	Friday	Saturday	Sunday
MALES	☑Stretch ☑Push-ups/ Sit-ups: 1 minute X 4 sets each ☑Run: 20 minutes @ 7:45/mile	☑Stretch ☑Calisthenics: 30-minute circuit ☑Stretch	☑Stretch ☑Run; Intervals: ¼ mile sprint ¼ mile jog X 4 each ☑Stretch	☑Active Rest: Light activity and stretching twice during the day -or- Ruck: 3-5 miles @ 2-3 mph	☑Calisthenics: 30-minute circuit ☑Run: 30 minutes @ 8:30/ mile ☑Stretch	☑Stretch ☑Ruck: 3-5 miles @ 2-3 mph pace	No activity
FEMALES	☑Stretch ☑Push-ups/ Sit-ups: 1 minute X 4 sets each ☑Run: 20 minutes @ 9:30/mile	☑Stretch ☑Calisthenics: 30-minute circuit ☑Stretch	☑Stretch ☑Run; Intervals: ¼ mile sprint ¼ mile jog X 4 each ☑Stretch	☑Active Rest: Light activity and stretching twice during the day -or- Ruck: 3-5 miles @ 2-3 mph	☑Calisthenics: 30-minute circuit ☑Run: 30 minutes @ 10:00/mile ☑Stretch	☑Stretch ☑Ruck: 3-5 miles @ 2-3 mph pace	No activity

Tracking and Evaluating Your Progress

If you're like me, you're pretty busy with everyday life, and it can be hard to remember what exactly you did from day to day. This is especially true with physical fitness. I still keep an exercise journal so that I can track of what I did and when I did it. My journal doesn't lie to me. If I think it's been two days since I last ran, but my journal says it's been four, then it's been four days since I last ran. Keep yourself honest in your fitness endeavors by tracking what, where, and how much you did on a calendar. There's no need to go into great detail when you document your training. It's strictly meant as a reminder, keeping you on the right path to your fitness goals.

In the previous section, I outline the way to self-evaluate your progress by performing the APFT no more often than once per month. This assessment will give you the feedback required to know how well you're progressing in your fitness outline and what you need to change or modify. For example, if your two-mile run time is getting better but your push-ups and sit-ups are not improving, then you'll need to modify your training routine to include more of those exercises. Having a friend or your Recruiter keep time and evaluate your form during your APFT is important to ensure proper form, leading to an accurately graded test.

Other Sources of Physical Fitness Information

As I've mentioned before, there is plenty of great information in cyberspace that can offer you individualized training routines based on where you are and where you need to be.

A few of the more reliable Web-sites that offer free, well-balanced fitness advice are: www.runnersworld.com; www.mensfitness. com; www.womenshealthmag.com. Each Web-site is based on its respective magazine and offers archived articles, which will most likely contain a topic of interest to you.

★   **The Pocket Physical Training Guide**

The Army has a well-written and comprehensive fitness manual called the *Pocket Physical Training Guide.* Compiled and written by the U.S. Army Physical Fitness School (USAPFS) and printed by the U.S. Government Printing Office (USGPO), it is intended to be used as a preparatory physical fitness guide for BCT. The manual serves as a recruitment aid and is provided free-of-charge to soldiers.

Not only is this good overall fitness guidance, but the illustrated and outlined exercises make up the components of the conditioning and stretch drills that you will be performing while at BCT. The guide also contains a twelve-week conditioning program that progresses according to your current fitness level and encompasses each component of physical fitness: muscular strength, muscular endurance, flexibility, and cardiovascular conditioning. If you make the effort and follow this program, you'll transform into a PT stud (or studette).

The Army's Pocket Physical Training Guide.

The only way to obtain a copy of the printed and bound version of the book is through your Recruiter or a career counselor at MEPS. However, an electronic version is available as a free download from the Internet.

Visit my Web site, *www.63daysandawakeup.com*, and click on the "Physical Training" link. There, you'll see a link for the guidebook and other physical fitness-related links, including downloadable videos demonstrating the different physical conditioning drills that you'll find in the manual. All of it is free to you, so take advantage of it.

Appendix C:
I.C.E. Sheet

Soldier-in-Training Contingency and Contact Form
In Case of Emergency (ICE) Sheet

The In Case of Emergency (ICE) sheet contains important contact information for your family about you while you're in training. Some of this form can be filled out now, but you'll have to wait until you arrive at BCT to add your contact information in order for it to be complete.

The full-size, printable version of this form is available as a free download from my Web site, www.63daysandawakeup.com.

SOLDIER PERSONAL CONTACT INFORMATION				
Name:		SSN:		DOB:
BCT/AIT Mailing Address:				
Training Site:		Battalion:	Company:	Platoon:
Commanding Officer:		Company NCOIC:		
Company Mailing Address:				
Phone Number: ( ) -				

RECRUITER CONTACT INFORMATION		
Recruiter Name:	E-Mail Address:	
Mailing Address:		
Office Phone: ( ) -	Cell Phone: ( ) -	Pager Number: ( ) -

IN CASE OF EMERGENCY (ICE)	
American Red Cross: National; (800) 922-4469	Local Chapter; ( ) -

In order to reach your soldier in case of family emergency, you'll need to contact the American Red Cross (ARC) at the above number, or contact your local chapter. The ARC will need the information in the SOLDIER PERSONAL CONTACT INFORMATION section to notify your soldier through their chain of command.

If you are having trouble contacting ARC, or you need additional assistance, contact your soldiers' Recruiter.

EMERGENCY MEDICAL INFORMATION	
Medications:	Blood Type:
Allergies to Medicines:	Religious Preference:
Other Pertinent Medical History/Information:	

The Army will have a file containing your soldier's health information, which will be referenced in case of a medical emergency or injury during training. However, it's a good idea to have this information handy in case the medical file is separated from the main personnel file.

Visit Us on the Web!
www.63daysandawakeup.com

Author Contact Information ★ Physical Fitness Advice ★ Book Updates ★ BCT Resources

AudioBook Download

Purchase, download, and listen to the book in either MP3 or WMA format. Listen on your PC, or transfer it to your portable audio player.

AudioBook On CD

Purchase the AudioBook on CD and listen anywhere, anytime.

★Free Downloads★

The Army Pocket Physical Training Guide is your one-stop guidance source for getting into "Army Shape".

Download a printable version of the Know-Go Card; a valuable study guide which can be folded into a pocket-sized reference.

Download the printable full-size version of this important personalized form for your family to have while you're away at BCT. Print new one's off as you need them for AIT and beyond.

About the Author

Don Herbert is a Health Care Specialist (MOS 68W) with the Michigan Army National Guard. In the spring of 2006, at the age of thirty-eight, he enlisted in the Army, attending BCT at Fort Jackson, South Carolina, and AIT at Fort Sam, Houston, Texas. He is a full-time firefighter/critical care paramedic with Independence Fire Department in Clarkston, Michigan and has been in the fire service since 1988.

His educational background is in health, fitness, and medicine. His military education travels will eventually take him to the Army Interservice Physician Assistant Program (IPAP). His writings have appeared in trade publications and on opinion pages across the country. He occasionally speaks at educational conferences and is considered an authority on the subject of firefighter fitness and health.

SPC Herbert resides in preferred relative anonymity with his wife and children in Davison, Michigan. He spends his free time at home de-skunking his dog, rewinding Sponge Bob videos, locating foul odors in his three-year-old's bedroom, and pleading with his neighbor to wear clothes while shooting groundhogs in his backyard. Don is available for speaking engagements, book signings, ice cream socials, coffee klatches, or to take unwanted Detroit Red Wings tickets off your hands. He can be reached by email at don@63daysandawakeup.com.

If you ever have the chance to meet him, please don't insult his dog. His wife and kids, however, are fair game.

978-0-595-42511-2
0-595-42511-9

Made in the USA
San Bernardino, CA
28 February 2013